In Memoriam

The Captain

Contents

Acknowledgments

Dominator and I must thank Jerry "Stickman" and John "Skinny" for their amazing help in writing this book. Stickman did countless computer simulations over hundreds of hours, along with mathematical analysis, in order to prove our radical new betting theories. Skinny helped me phrase and analyze the revelatory sections on "dice flipping." Not only are these two men magnificent controlled dice shooters, but they are also good friends and deserve applause for contributing their genius to this book. Thank you guys for everything that you have done!

CHAPTER 1

The Worrywart

I'm worried about this book. It is designed for serious craps players and for those shooters who have developed a controlled throw and/or are looking to advance their game considerably. This book concentrates on advantage play—in short, play that allows players to get the edge over the house. You want to become a real threat to the casinos? Then this book is for you. In it, you can go from being a savvy, smart craps player or an advantage player with a slight edge over the house to being a dynamo that will be the casinos' worst nightmare.

This is definitely not a primer book on betting systems for the millions of craps players laboring under the superstition that they can find some magic betting formula to beat the *random game* of craps, and it doesn't explain how the game is played for those of you who are novices. You should know the game of craps before you read this book. You should be good at it, comfortable playing it. In fact, I hope you are great at it. If you want to get the full background to proper craps play, I refer you to *Casino Craps: Shoot to Win!* (Triumph Books), which teaches everything you need to know about the game and also how to control the dice. That book is also accompanied by a DVD that shows you how to make controlled shots.

My major worry is that the truly advanced concepts in this book will be used by the wrong players—the novice dice controllers and, sadly, those "unadvanced" players known pejoratively as *gamblers*. Golden Touch Craps, the premier dice-control school in the country, teaches a strict form of dice control based on techniques first formulated by the Captain, the greatest craps expert who ever lived and a man who once

1

rolled 147 numbers before he sevened out—and these techniques actually work in the casinos, as our students have discovered.

Just as important as a controlled throw, advantage craps players need a very strict betting style to be successful. They must make the lowest-house-edge bets that fit into their mathematical edge as determined by their SRR (seven-to-rolls ratio) and also upon an on-axis analysis given by the software program SmartCraps.

Players who have an SRR that shows a change from randomness know they are changing the nature of the game. Players who have a greater-than-random on-axis control are also changing the nature of the game in *radical* ways. With an edge shown by your SRR and/or an edge established by SmartCraps, you know you can beat the game of craps if you bet properly—and betting properly might just be different depending on how you are analyzing your edge over the house.

Are SRR and axis control the alpha and omega of dice control? No... and yes. The SRR is a decent indicator of control; it tells you that you have the goods to change the probabilities of the game, while the SmartCraps program is a much stronger indicator because it establishes that you have on-axis control. A low SRR with a high on-axis control is better than a high SRR with no on-axis control. Still, a good SRR of 1:6.5 or higher means the game of craps can be yours. But these indicators—strong or weak—are just indicators. You actually have to go into the casino and play the game. Ultimately, over a sufficiently long period of time, you should have more money in your pocket or purse than when you started. As we say in Golden Touch Craps (hereafter referred to as *GTC*), "Winning is the most fun!"

In the short run of any game you will have losses; unfortunately that is inevitable. But to be an advantage craps player you must show that you can actually beat the casinos. You must show you can bring home the money; otherwise you are conning yourself into believing you are good at advantage play when you are really not. However, there is an interesting subset to beating the house. Many readers and viewers of our GTC materials just don't practice enough to develop a controlled throw that beats the game. Yet, they nevertheless have improved their game immensely by simply following our strong betting strategies, which include the 5-Count and proper low-house-edge wagers. That's good not great, but good is far better than bad.

Indeed, in this book, for the first time in print, we will show how the 5-Count actually can change the nature of craps into a positive expectation at certain times. Even non-controlled shooters can take advantage of this element in the GTC advanced betting arsenal. The 5-Count is a revolution that keeps on giving. Once again, thank you, Captain, for discovering the amazing 5-Count. In the Appendix of this book you will find the 5-Count section originally printed in *Casino Craps: Shoot to Win!*

Are most of the ideas in this book advanced? Yes. Should they be played against random shooters who just wing the dice down the table? No. In fact, if you can avoid betting on all random shooters, the better off you will be.

We also have some strategies that are radical—*highly* radical—that might blow the lid off advanced craps betting. Did I just write "might"? Sorry, these radical bets will *definitely* blow the lid off advanced craps betting. These radical methods will include a new and brilliant method of betting for those who show truly superior on-axis control, a method the great dice controller Dominator and many other elite (I repeat, *elite*) GTC bettors have been using with great success for a few years.

Some of you who have seen Dominator use these methods have said to me, "But you teach *this* thing in class, but he is doing *that*. What gives?" I usually skirt this issue by saying that Dominator has too much of the gambler still in him, so he sometimes goes a little overboard in his betting style. In truth, this is not entirely accurate because some of his methods actually bring home more money than the regular GTC betting methods would—but these methods are only for truly advanced on-axis-controlled players. If you don't have that elite level of on-axis control, you'll be putting your head in the guillotine using our radical methods.

Sadly too many decent dice controllers are of the opinion that they are *great* dice controllers. That assumption can be fraught with danger for such dice controllers' bankrolls. If you attempt to use our new and radical methods of betting and you aren't at the necessary level of skill, your bankroll will be creamed along with your ego. So I caution everyone reading this: When in doubt, figure you aren't as good a shooter in the casinos as you are at home. And, just to be cautious, figure you aren't as good a shooter as you think you are, period. Take yourself down a peg, and if you still see that you have the ability to play the radical way, then go for it...at least for a long enough period of time to actually see if you are pulling off these radical betting methods.

Next, part of being a skilled dice controller includes your mental state while playing. If you've ever been an athlete, you know how important your mind is for success. You can have all the physical skill in the world, but if your mind is not properly trained your body will probably not do what you have conditioned it to do. With that in mind (pun intended) I have written a chapter that will teach you both visualization and meditation techniques. These are designed to give you the mental edge to go along with your physical edge. Indeed, even if you aren't an advantage player, these techniques are in and of themselves good to learn because a trained mind is important in every aspect of life.

Finally, Dominator and I had a serious decision to make before writing this book—how many of the advanced graphs, charts, and other mathematical diagrams to ladle onto our pages. Everything we are going to discuss in this book is proven, either through math or through computer simulations. Dom, the other elite GTC shooters, and I have done everything that we are going to share with you, and we've done it all in the heat of battle in the casinos. There is no pie-in-the-sky wishful thinking coming up. Still, did we want endless reams of figures for those few mathletes who enjoy poring over such things?

I've read craps writers and other gambling writers who pour so many statistics and charts into their articles and books that normal people, such as me and you, find them distracting as opposed to enlightening. I find that I often skip those parts due to their redundancy. Of course, I am not talking about gambling's phony systems sellers who create bizarre constructs but rather about those solid writers who just can't pull themselves away from their abacuses.

So we will give you the math and simulations to show we are correct in our advice, but we'll keep it to a useful minimum.

With all that in your hands, this book should take you to the next step in your knowledge and education about the game of craps. In fact, you might very well join the craps-playing elite.

Remember: "Winning is the most fun!"

Enjoy.

CHAPTER 2

Refresher Questions About the SRR, Money Management, and Advanced Play

Question: Just as a refresher, please explain the SRR and how it relates to dice control.

Answer: In a random game of craps, the 7 comes up six times for every 36 rolls or once every six rolls. Naturally that is a long-range average. In short-run play, the SRR can be all over the board, but over time the SRR will begin to give you a very good idea of what kind of edge you have over the house. So, again, the SRR is one 7 for every six rolls, or 1:6. If a shooter can start to reduce the appearance of the 7 to 1:6.3 or better, he can get an edge at the game. The better the SRR, the higher the player's edge will be over the game; that is the theory of the SRR. Players can also have "negative" SRRs of 1:5.8 or lower. Of course, to establish your SRR and to have any confidence in it, you must do at least several thousand rolls of the dice.

Question: You say "theory," but isn't it true?

Answer: It is true, but there are some caveats to using the SRR as the only tool for analyzing your shot. In our classes we stress that the SRR is an important tool but is not the only or perhaps even the best tool to establish your edge over the game.

When we speak in general about the SRR, we tend to use the shorthand that all the other numbers are proportionally increased in their appearance as the 7 is decreased. This is probably not so. Some faces will probably come up more; some will come up less. If you have a high SRR but tend to hit a lot of garbage numbers—such as 2, 3, 11, and 12—that SRR is not as powerful as you might think. So you have to judge the power of your SRR the best way you can—how you are actually doing in casino play. New players, though, can use the SRR as a confidence booster. As your SRR goes up, you know you are exercising influence over the dice. That is the first and main step in the development of a competent dice controller.

Question: If the garbage numbers come up, should you bet those?

Answer: No. For most players betting the high-house-edge bets is an invitation for disaster. The chances of having an edge over those numbers would be remote for most controlled shooters if all you are using is your SRR. You don't want to try to overcome edges that are often in the double digits merely based on your SRR. You have to be very careful using the SRR to allow you to attempt overcoming high-house-edge bets.

Question: Does every controlled shooter's SRR keep going up?

Answer: Most do, at least early on, but some don't. In practice, if you start out like a ball of fire, it is possible that your bloated SRR will be reduced after you've done thousands or tens of thousands of rolls. On the flip side, if you have a low SRR in the beginning of your practice, it is highly possible that your SRR will increase over time as you get better and better at controlling the dice. This seems to be a general pattern in the development of a winning SRR, although in groupings of numbers you will see startling discrepancies in SRR results, much like baseball hitters go in and out of good and bad streaks. But over time, the SRR gives you a decent indication that you have developed the dice-control skill. From that point on you will probably want to work on your on-axis control, which can be judged by the SmartCraps software program.

Question: What is a decent SRR?

Answer: If you get between 1:6.5 and 1:6.8 you are now truly capable of beating the game of craps—if you make the right bets. You cannot make crazy crapper bets in the middle of the table, or the Field bet, or silly bets such as the Horn and the Whirl/World. You are also much better off making Come bets with odds than you are Placing the box numbers in most cases. Here is a small example of what kind of edges you can get, assuming an equal distribution of numbers, which is probably not the case in reality. But at least looking at these charts will help you see how your edge goes up with an increase in your SRR. Please note how the increase in Odds on the Pass and Come bets really propel those house edges in the shooter's favor.

Place Bet	*SRR*
6 and 8	1:6.2
5 and 9	1:6.5
4 and 10	1:6.7
Buy 5 and 9 at $30 with vig $1 on win only	1:6.2
Buy 4 and 10 for $25 with vig $1 on win only	1:6.2

Pass and Come	*Your Edge*	*Your Edge*	*Your Edge*	*Your Edge*	*Your Edge*
SRR	No Odds	1X Odds	2X Odds	5X Odds	10X Odds
1:6.5	1.6 %	3.3 %	4 %	4.8 %	5.2 %
1:7	4.5 %	7.1 %	8.2 %	9.5 %	10.1 %
1:8	9.5 %	14 %	15.8 %	17.9 %	19 %

Question: What would be the best way to bet a decent SRR?

Answer: When you are shooting, one way is to do a Pass Line bet and two Come bets with Odds or a Pass Line bet with the placing of the 6 and 8. At a 5X odds game (or better) you are probably better off with just Pass Line and Come bets. Do not allow yourself to get into the dementia that can occur at a craps table as you see gamblers hitting high-house-edge bets. You are merely seeing a little window when you are at the table, and those hopeless gamblers exist outside that window too. Those poor saps playing a random game of craps who make the high-house-edge bets are long-term losers, no matter what you are seeing at that moment. They have to be; they are playing a negative-expectation game. For controlled shooters who do not have strong on-axis control (next chapter), using the Come will get you on numbers we wouldn't recommend you Place-bet, such as the 5, 9, 4, and 10. Keep in mind that just because a random shooter has hit a bunch of Crazy Crapper bets, that does not mean he will continue to hit those bets, because he has no control over the dice. You are just watching randomness in action when a random roller shoots those bones. He is no different from a slot machine's RNG (random-number generator), which makes the slots a random game as well.

Question: Do controlled shooters win most times they shoot?

Answer: A major myth in the world of dice control is that a controlled shooter wins most times when he or she gets the dice. Except for the Arm—a woman who was the greatest dice controller of all time, whose eccentric throw seems not to be duplicable and who won the majority of the time when she got the dice—we have never met a good or even elite dice controller who wins most times when he or she gets the dice. Hard though this is to believe, most turns with the dice will be losers.

To use a baseball analogy, dice controllers are .300 to .400 hitters, but their wins more than make up for their losses. People who play at the tables with elite GTC shooters are sometimes disappointed that every hand by one of them isn't a winner. It would have been nice if Babe Ruth could hit a home run every time he came to the plate, but that just doesn't happen. However, dice controllers do tend to have many more long rolls, some even monster hands of 30, 40, 50, 60, 70, or 80 numbers before sevening out. Check our world records page on the Internet at www.goldentouchcraps.com. Don't get fooled by false advertising or craps gurus who claim they can make you win almost every time you take the dice. These folks are simply taking you for ploppies.

Even more important for long-term profits are the small wins, usually associated with repeating numbers. Keep in mind, truly bad rolls—those point/seven outs—can only lose you those initial bets. So the many times you have winners on short rolls of repeating numbers will contribute more income to your bankroll than those occasional monsters, although naturally those monsters are the truly fun ones to write and brag about.

Question: Does your dice-control edge stay stable over time?

Answer: In a random game of craps all the numbers are stagnant, and the edges remain the same on the first roll, the hundredth roll, the trillionth roll. But when you deal with skill, your edge will increase or decrease as time passes. How should this affect your betting? If you are a relative novice or intermediate player without strong on-axis control, then you should be betting the best bets (that goes without saying), but your bets must be pegged to your bankroll, *not* what you perceive as your skill level. Arrogance over one's perceived edge is dangerous. Yes, we know some dice gurus like to postulate that people have the same edges over time, but this isn't so. Edges ebb and flow and ebb and flow some more. That is the very nature of a skill game—the ebb and the flow.

No one could have predicted how many home runs Babe Ruth would hit in his career. Prophecy is not in the cards...or dice...in skill games—except to say, "I do have an edge, I will win money, but my edge and my wins will change from this time to that time." Overbetting can be a killer of your bankroll. Yes, you might be underbetting too, but that just slows your winning down; it can't destroy you like overbetting can. If you continue to see a high SRR and you see your bankroll increasing, then your bets should increase in proportion as well. It is very difficult to establish stagnant SRRs of this or that percent, because in skill activities many things will come into play in the short run. I'll discuss these later in the book.

Question: What are the limits to the SRR? If you change your dice set doesn't it change the SRR?

Answer: The technical answer is yes. New dice set, new SRR. Some dice sets are really anti-seven sets, with the Hardway set being the best of them. Other sets such as 3V and 2V are not as friendly to the anti-seven goal, but these sets are strong when you have good on-axis control. So for the purposes of establishing whether you are changing the nature of the game, the set to use to establish a verifiable edge is the Hardway set. If SmartCraps, our software analysis program, tells you to use an on-axis-friendly set, such as 3V, then you can switch since your on-axis performance indicates better money-making opportunities with a different set. Can you be an advanced shooter without great on-axis control?

Yes. The Hardway set allows for various flips and flops of the dice when they land without hitting that dreaded 7. You do not have to be a strong axis-control shooter to gain dice-control skill and beat the casino.

Question: What is "below" or "worse than" random?
Answer: Below random is the mistaken idea that something can be less than random. A dice throw is either random or controlled. There is no such thing as less than random or more than random. We sometimes use the phrase "worse than random" in this book as slang, but it is not to be taken literally. It just means it is an SRR under 1:6 as opposed to over 1:6—though both are controlled throws.

Question: What percentage of your bankroll should you bet at craps?
Answer: This is an easy question to ask and a hard question to answer. Many players can bet 10 percent of $1,000 and it has no influence on their emotional state when shooting. That same person cannot bet 10 percent of $10,000, because a $1,000 bet scares him. The percentages are the same, but for many players money has an absolute value, not a relative one.

Is the absolute sense of money the best framework for betting? No. Absolutes can stifle you, but nevertheless these are real feelings and have to be handled. Simply saying, "Don't feel this absolute sense of money," as many gambling writers do, won't stop you from feeling it. If betting $1,000 makes you think, *God, I am betting $1,000!* before you throw, then you are not in your rolling zone, and more than likely you are just a random roller at that moment. So that is the first step. Are you able to bet in percentages without qualm? If yes, then use percentages. If your bankroll increases, no matter how high it increases, bet the same percentage.

What percentage should that be? Since I am really conservative, I would say that you should bet 1 percent of your total bankroll initially (I bet one-tenth of one percent!). So if your bankroll is $1,000, you bet $10. If your bankroll is $10,000, you bet $100; $50,000, you bet $500; and so on. Players with higher risk tolerances can adjust these percentages to their comfort zones. You really have to determine this for yourself.

But don't fool yourself into thinking you have a higher risk tolerance than you actually have. Going on big losing streaks, which most dice controllers will inevitably experience, can knock your deluded sense of high risk tolerance right out the window. I've seen this in my investment activities. Many of my friends will tell their investment agents that they have a real high tolerance for risk, but when their portfolio starts heading downhill, their self-assessed risk tolerance suddenly lowers to an almost no-risk policy.

For those who have an absolute sense of money and can't get rid of this feeling over time, they should do the percentage thing until they hit the wall. If the wall of absolutism stops you from betting more, so be it. Your bankroll will go up anyway, although not quite as fast. The worst thing a controlled shooter can do is think of the money being wagered while he shoots. That's a loss waiting to happen. You have to play this game as if the chips on the layout are meaningless.

Question: How do you define bankroll?
Answer: I recommend that you have a separate money-market account for gambling. We call this the 401G (the *G* stands for "gambling"). Whatever money you have in that account is your bankroll. You only bet in accordance with that amount. Have your 401G in an interest-bearing account such as a money-market account where you will make some money even when you are not playing at the craps tables.

Question: Should you use session bankrolls?
Answer: Gamblers should use session bankrolls; advantage players shouldn't. As an advantage craps player you stop playing when you feel a sense of fatigue or you take three to four turns with the dice and you look awful or—even if you are winning—you notice that your dice actually don't look so good. Then it is time to take a break. The fatigue of shooting dice is real. It isn't the fatigue of working out in the gym, but when you shoot you are concentrating, and that concentration can have a draining effect. If you are losing during a session, such a draining effect can be amplified in some players. So session bankrolls are out and body awareness is in! If all else fails, memorize this saying: "When in doubt, get out." My personal mantra is, "I gamble with one foot pointed toward the door."

Question: Should you have win goals and loss limits?

Answer: If you know you are going to shoot the dice four times in a given session (unless you are hotter than Hades), then your loss limit is already set. Just multiply four times your initial bet spread on one hand. If you are betting $50, then your loss limit is $200. You will have to include what you are betting on random rollers who make it past the 5-Count, but these sums should be very small. There are no win goals, only an understanding of your fatigue level. Sometimes after a long roll, fatigue can set in quickly. That adrenaline rush while you were shooting will drain away rather fast after the big roll is over. That might be your win goal right there.

Question: In dice control, as in blackjack, don't things all even out based on your edge?

Answer: In the long run, for blackjack, the answer is yes. Blackjack is strictly a statistical game despite the fact that getting an edge through card counting is a skill. Keep an accurate count of the cards, and the statistics are stagnant. All the aces come out, there will be no blackjacks. Your counting skills do not change that one bit.

A random craps game is stagnant in a simpler way. The probabilities are set in stone from the outset. But in dice control, while we would like to think all things even out over the long run, they actually don't. Indeed, things *uneven* out. Since your skill changes the nature of the probabilities, a change in your skill levels will change the degree of your edge. Yesterday, you were feeling great; the dice looked great, landed great, and died great; and you killed the casino. Last night you hurt your hand a little while performing karaoke in a drunken haze at a nightclub before you had to be carted to your room, and today your dice looked bad, landed poorly, bounced like crazy off the back wall, and the casino killed you. One day your skill was at one level; the next day your skill was at another level.

Being a wise bettor, yesterday when your skill was at its peak you took the dice several times to maximize your wins. When you stunk, you took the dice twice and got the hell out of there. So many variables affect your play as a dice controller that you really can't narrow down your edge to one percentage or even a set of percentages in real casinos.

At home, using the same practice equipment, you can get a good read as to whether or not you are a competent dice controller or an elite one.

Think of the myriad things that can affect your skill levels. Getting older might make you worse...or it might make you better because money has less meaning to you since you have more of it. Your eyes might get weaker and your arms might get arthritis. The greatest shooter of all time, the Arm, had to quit shooting when she became crippled with severe arthritis. Had she kept shooting, her edge would probably have disappeared and she would have become one of the millions of random rollers.

There is no fully accurate assessment of what your edge is in the casinos—except that with practice, keeping records of your throws (especially in the beginning) and winning money in the casinos tells you clearly you do have an edge. Your at-home percentages are extremely helpful in giving you confidence, and your overall casino performance will give you even more confidence because money won equates with confidence. The passing of the SmartCraps tests will tell you that you have good on-axis control, and this puts you in a more elite category of player.

But as an advanced player, don't get stuck in the edge dilemma. You know you are good, so take it from there.

Question: Are there radical betting styles for decent SRRs and really good SRRs?

Answer: In general the answer is a resounding no! There is a tendency that when SRRs start to get over 1:7 and hit 1:8 or higher we see more and more on-axis control over the dice. Using the Hardway set of 2:2, 4:4, 5:5, and 3:3, we shall start to see these faces appearing more and more and also appearing more and more closely to the primary Hardway set we are using—in short we'll start to see more Hardway numbers. Once on-axis control gets well past the random 44.4 on-axis percentage the dice controller has now entered a different competitive arena—his or her edge now has specific meaning in terms of what faces and what numbers can be purposely thrown with some precision. Here new betting styles and new dice sets could be in the offing—some of these quite radical.

CHAPTER 3

On-Axis Control and Radical Betting Styles

The Five Horsemen—Dominator, Stickman, Skinny, Nick-at-Night, and I—are at the craps table, and Dom has just gotten the dice. There are several GTC dice-control students at the table as well, students we have recently taught to control the dice and bet properly. Without proper low-house-edge bets, dice control will be a losing proposition for these new shooters. That's what we teach. That's what we hammer home into the minds of gamblers trying to become advantage craps players. Eschew the Crazy Crapper bets such as the Hop bets; the Horn; the Whirl; the Yo-Eleven; the craps numbers of 2, 3, and 12; and the hard 4, 6, 8, and 10. Stick with Pass Line and Come bets with Odds. Just Place the 6 and 8 and buy the 4 and 10 for $25 or $50 if the commission is only taken on wins.

Proper betting is our mantra. We believe in it fully—with our whole hearts, minds, and spirits.

Except...

Dom establishes his point, and then he throws out a green $25 chip and yells, "Hop the hard 6!" The faces of the students are stunned. You can practically hear them thinking, *What the heck is Dominator doing? Didn't he constantly lecture us on betting only the best house-edge bets? Now he's throwing out a bet with a house edge of over 11 percent. What the heck is going on?*

Of course, as almost always happens, the students take me aside. "Frank, what was Dom doing? He goes nuts in class saying to make the best bets and to follow the math, and now he plays like a wild man. Yeah, he hit some of those bets, but that was just luck, right? I mean, who can overcome those high house edges to make those bets worthwhile to do? Isn't he a hypocrite?"

I am at a loss for words during these times because I actually don't want to open Pandora's box by telling the truth, which will be misinterpreted by eager novice and intermediate dice controllers whose on-axis control is more or less random and who will kill their bankrolls if they try to bet like Dominator. So I say, "Well, Dom has that gambler in him. Ignore the bets and do what we teach in class." It's the old "I may smoke, but you shouldn't" lesson many parents have attempted to teach their children.

Okay, so now I am going to blow the lid off my past prevarications. Dominator and other elite dice controllers whose on-axis control is way above random can actually make more money from some Crazy Crapper bets than they can from placing those same numbers. That's right. With a proper understanding of where you stand in terms of your on-axis dice-control ability, you can consider making some of these otherwise ridiculous bets, which will now give you a much greater *mathematical edge* over the house than the low-house-edge bets.

Oh, my Lord, this is true—it is the *reversal* of everything we teach in our classes, for the elite on-axis shooters that is. These advanced shooters must also decide whether they want to shift from the Hardway set to another set such as the 3V, 2V, Straight 6s, etc. If you are an advanced or elite shooter, then you have to decide if these new radical betting styles should be incorporated into your game.

A word of caution here from Mr. Worrywart: Don't be foolish and think our strong advice about proper betting given in our classes and in our *Casino Craps: Shoot to Win!* book is now wrong. Using a radical style of betting is only for those of you who have proven your advanced on-axis skills by using the software program SmartCraps or by analyzing rolls using pen, paper, and math (or spreadsheets). Very few novice dice controllers will get to the point where they can be on-axis casino killers in a short time. So enjoy the knowledge in this chapter...but go slow, please go *slow*. If you hop on the bets I am going to discuss and your skill level is not up to it, you will kill your bankroll. So *judiciousness* is the key word here.

The following information was researched by Jerry "Stickman," who helped me write this chapter. Stickman is an elite shooter of the highest order. His on-axis control is amazing. Look at this string of numbers from one of his recent rolls: 4, 6, 6, 6, 6, 6, 6, 4, 6, 6, 9, 6, 6, 6, 10, 6, 6, 8, 6, 6, 6, 6, 8, 6, 6, 6, 6, 6, 7. I'd say a streak like that is damn good and damn rare for random rollers shooting those dice.

Strangely enough, when Stickman had this roll, some poor ploppy at the table said, "I never bet the six. It's an unlucky number." This poor sod actually lost money on Stickman's roll! You do see a lot of strange things at a craps table, that's for sure.

Stickman's string of in-casino rolls shows amazing on-axis control. Had it been merely a singular event, then it could be dismissed as merely the extreme side of normal variance. But Stickman, along with Dominator and many other advanced and elite shooters, is actually able to keep those dice on axis far more than probability indicates. In fact, for some of them their on-axis control is nothing short of spectacular.

Now let me ask the big question: Can one of the game's worst bets, the Hop bet, actually be a better-paying bet than placing the 6 and 8 or buying the 4 and 10 at $25 and $50 with commissions paid on wins only, which are two of the best Place bets in the game of craps? Can the horrible Hop bet be better than these for advanced on-axis shooters? Can you get a better mathematical edge on the Hop bets than you can on the best possible Place bets? Let's see. Dice controllers, your world is about to be rocked!

Anyone who knows the math of the game of craps knows that the Pass Line and Come bets with Odds are the best bets to make in a random game. They also know that placing the 6 and 8 are also good bets with a relatively small 1.52 percent house edge. Among the worst bets available in craps are Hop bets. They are horrible bets in the random game—like vampire bets for your bankroll—and they will bleed a bettor dry.

A Hop bet is a wager on what the next roll of the dice will show— not just the total of the dice but which pips will appear on each die. Examples: a total of 6 can be made with 1:5, 5:1, 2:4, 4:2, and 3:3. In a random game over time, any one of these combinations would appear once in 36 rolls. That makes the odds against winning a bet on one of these specific Hop bet results 35-to-1, as there are 35 ways to lose and only one way to win. The casino typically pays 30-to-1, severely short-changing the payout to make its profit by creating an abominable edge against the player. This gives the casino a 13.89 percent house edge in a random game on such Hop bets, which is absolutely rotten.

Casinos cannot distinguish between a result of 5:1 and 1:5 since they do not keep track of which pip has shown from which die (dice of the same color can't really be followed in a normal game). Thus, there are two types of Hop bets for the 6—those that can occur "two ways"—such as the 1:5 or 5:1 and the 2:4 or 4:2—and those that can occur only one way, such as 3:3. The true odds against throwing a two-way result—such as 1:5/5:1—are 34-to-2, meaning 34 ways to lose and two ways to win, or 17-to-1. The casino pays 15-to-1 on this bet for a house edge of 11.11 percent, another ghastly bet in the random game.

It is clear that in a random game one should stay away from Hop bets and only bet the lower-house-edge bets as we recommend in our primer and refresher classes. Since advanced on-axis controlled shooters can change the nature of the game, conventional wisdom may no longer apply. In fact, such wisdom might have to be thrown out the window.

Could a controlled shooter ever get good enough that it would benefit him more to bet a Hop bet rather than placing the 6 or 8? The initial reaction may be for one to think, *The house edge is the house edge, and we should bet only the lowest house edge.* This is mostly true for almost all players. But let's dig a little deeper.

The Golden Touch controlled throw is designed to ultimately keep the dice on axis, although our recommended Hardway set is also designed to allow the non-axis results to be advantageous to the controlled shooter. Using the Hardway set—where the one-pips and the six-pips are put on-axis (outside left and right of the dice set)—the better the controlled shooter keeps the dice on axis, then the less the 1s and 6s will appear.

If a shooter could keep the dice on axis on *every* throw, the 1-pip or 6-pip would *never* appear. That means certain results would never appear. Without a 6-pip, we would never throw an 11 or 12 or a 6:2 or 6:1 and so on. Without a 1-pip, we would never throw the numbers 2 or 3 or a 5:1 for the number 6 or 4:1 for the number 5, and so on. The nature of the game is indeed changed by perfect on-axis results—radically changed, in fact.

Now suppose that not only are the dice on axis every throw but that the controlled shooter also has 100 percent pitch control. In other words, he is *perfect!* Using the Hardway set, a perfect throw would result in *only* Hardway numbers being rolled: 2:2, 3:3, 4:4, and 5:5. So let's assume this perfect thrower uses the Hardway set and only throws hard 4s, 6s, 8s, and 10s. If this shooter places the hard 6 (3:3) for $10, he will hit it one out of four times, as the 3:3 is one of four Hardway sides. He will win $90 on the one winning roll at 9-to-1. He will lose $30 on the three losing rolls of 2:2, 4:4, and 5:5. So his net win is $60. The winning hard 6 bet returns 600 percent for every four rolls. If, however, this perfect shooter makes a $10 Hop bet on the 3:3, he will also win the bet one out of four rolls. But since the 3:3 Hop bet pays 30-to-1, he will win $300 on the winning roll and lose $30 on the three losing rolls for a net win of $270. The winning Hop bet of 3:3 returns 2700 percent for every four rolls. Now, that is a monstrous improvement! With perfect on-axis throws, the house edge changes drastically on the Hop bets versus the Hardway bets. The Hop bet becomes the preferred bet for the perfect shooter.

Of course perfection is an unachievable goal in the real world of dice control, even for the most elite shooters in the world. But there are advanced and elite shooters whose on-axis control is good enough that Hop bets do become recommended bets for them.

So how do things change as a controlled shooter gets better and better at keeping the dice on axis? Is there a point where it becomes more advantageous betting a hopping 3:3 than actually placing the 6? (These results would also prove to be the same when using the number 8.) Let's look at some examples of different degrees of dice control and their effect on placing the 6 or hopping a 3:3 by using the SmartCraps software program.

SmartCraps is a great program that does several things for the would-be on-axis dice controller. It will let you know if you are actually controlling the dice in such a fashion. If you are, it will tell you what your actual edge is using any dice set. It will tell you what the best dice sets are for winning Pass Line bets or hitting specific numbers. It also allows you to simulate any betting system for any level of dice control. That means you can see for yourself what different betting systems will produce for your specific level of skill. This is obviously a very helpful program for on-axis dice controllers.

To answer our Place bet versus Hop bet question, we only need two very simple betting schemes: placing a 6 for $6 or betting a hopping 3:3 for $6. We also must keep in mind that we are running a simulator, which simulates results by actually running millions of hands and determining the results. The results are subject to variances just like playing the actual game in the casinos. Depending on how many hands are simulated, the results could vary considerably from what the math of the game may indicate. However, the more hands that are simulated, the closer the results are to the mathematical model.

So let's look at a 10-million-hand simulation of dice hands, which produced the results presented here and in all of our chapters on betting. Even though these simulations may not precisely match the theoretical mathematical results, they are razor-edge close. The more decisions in a simulation, the closer the simulation comes to the math.

We first need a benchmark for our simulations—betting a hopping 3:3 and placing the 6 for a random shooter. If everything is correct, the simulations should show a 13.89 percent edge on hopping 3:3 and a 1.52 percent house edge for placing the 6. Our 10-million-hand simulation for the house edge of placing the 6 matches exactly with the theoretical math of 1.52 percent in a random game. The 3:3 Hop bet is within 0.06 percent of a random game at 13.83 percent. These percentages are reasonable and provide adequate validation of the simulator.

The next set of simulations was for someone who could *marginally* control the dice. Two simulations were run for each level of dice controller, one using the Hardway set and one using the 3V set, as these are the most common sets for a dice controller—especially when trying to hit a 6.

SmartCraps has three measures (or tests) to determine whether or not you have on-axis control of the dice. For this set of simulations the shooter just passed Test 1 (keeping the dice on axis—that is, the 2, 3, 4, and 5 will show), and for the other two SmartCraps tests we simply used random results. For the purposes of this study, 1,000 rolls were used as the roll set to make it easier to understand the simulation. This is a theoretical model to show percentages in a simple way. In the real world, 1,000 rolls is not a substantial enough number to make a good simulation.

In order to pass Test 1, a total of 482 rolls had to be on axis out of 1,000 rolls. That's 48.2 percent of the rolls being on axis as opposed to the 44.4 percent on-axis random rolls.

The other two tests are the number of primaries thrown—2:2, 3:3, 4:4, and 5:5 (Test 2) and the number of double-pitch 7s (5:2, 2:5, 4:3, and 3:4) (Test 3). These two SmartCraps tests only apply to those rolls that are on axis. In a game of random rolls, on-axis results only occur one-fourth with primaries and one-fourth with double pitches. Of the 482 on-axis rolls, 121 of them (or 12.1 percent) would be primaries and 121 (12.1 percent) would be double-pitch 7s. These are the numbers that were used for this set, and the results were quite interesting—to say the least.

We expected the edge of the game to move toward the player by either being a smaller house edge or possibly even a favorable edge for the shooter. Betting on the hopping 3:3 reduced the house edge against the player to about 6.26 percent for the Hardway set and about 6.17 percent for the 3V set. Both of these results moved the edge toward the player from random results as we expected—that is, from a house edge of 13.89 percent to a house edge slightly over 6 percent. Not bad but still losing bets for each set.

The results for Place betting the 6 did not follow the same pattern. These results were highly dependent on the set the shooter used. Using the 3V set, the on-axis controlled shooter had a 0.66 percent player edge versus the normal 1.52 percent edge for the house on placing the 6. However when using the Hardway set, a marginal on-axis dice controller actually did *worse*—increasing the house edge against the player to about 2.3 percent versus 1.52 percent! Wow! That could be considered shocking based on traditional thinking. The on-axis controlled shooter did far better with the 3V set than with the Hardway set. One got the edge over the casinos (the 3V), and one increased the edge of the casino over the player (the Hardway set).

For a random shooter, the dice set does not matter; in fact, nothing matters when the game is random except the traditional math. However, when there is some on-axis dice control, the dice set *does* matter for the results. Golden Touch recommends the Hardway set for the beginning dice controller because it provides the best protection against a 7, since very few novice shooters sufficiently keep the dice on axis. Indeed, most dice throws for novice and even intermediate players are extremely close to random in terms of on-axis control.

But once you have passed the SmartCraps tests that prove you are controlling the dice with superior on-axis performance, the program provides a recommended dice set. Since we are betting on the 6, the 3V set is usually the recommended set. The results of the marginal on-axis shooter using the Hardway set, while unexpected, point to the importance of knowing your on-axis dice-control skill and then using the SmartCraps recommended sets to achieve the correct winning results.

Even the marginal dice controller can gain an edge over the house by betting the proper bets and using the recommended set as evidenced by the approximately 0.6 percent player edge on placing the 6 using the 3V set.

Recommendation for Marginal On-Axis Results: *You should use the 3V set when placing the 6 and not use the Hardway set. You will get a slight edge over the house placing the 6 doing the 3V, while the Hardway set does the opposite and increases the house edge when placing the 6. Do not use any Hop bets even though the house edge has been lowered. These bets will still cripple your bankroll.*

The next four simulations were for an on-axis shooter who minimally passed all three SmartCraps tests. Placing the 6 and hopping the 3:3 were simulated with both the Hardway set and the 3V set with shocking results.

The specific numbers for this shooter were as follows: 1,000 total rolls, 482 rolls on axis, 144 primary hits, and 98 double-pitch 7s. So we are dealing with 48.2 percent on-axis rolls, 14.4 percent primary hits (2:2, 3:3, 4:4, and 5:5), and 0.98 percent double pitches.

In this set of simulations, all the results were positive for the shooter. The 3V set performed slightly better than the Hardway set.

Hardway Set Results:

Placing the 6 has a *player edge* of 7.6 percent.

Hopping the 3:3 has a *player edge* of 11.9 percent.

3V Set Results:

Placing the 6 has a *player edge* of 8.9 percent.

Hopping the 3:3 has a *player edge* of 11.6 percent.

What a difference passing all three of the SmartCraps tests makes! By just *marginally* passing all three SmartCraps tests, you can turn the house edges upside down. It is now more profitable for you to bet the hopping 3:3 than simply placing the 6—better by more than 30 percent!

Now let's look at what happens if the shooter can keep the dice on axis 50 percent of the time. Using the standard 1,000-roll set, this shooter will have 500 rolls on axis (50 percent) and merely the *random percentage* of hits for the other two SmartCraps tests—which are 125 each (12.5 percent). Here are the results:

Hardway Set Results:

Placing the 6 has a *house edge* of about 2.4 percent.

Hopping the 3:3 has a *house edge* of about 2.7 percent.

3V Set Results:

Placing the 6 has a **player edge** of about 1.7 percent.

Hopping the 3:3 has a *house edge* of about 3 percent.

Again, placing the 6 and using the Hardway set has results that are actually "worse" than in a random game. In fact the results for this shooter using the same bet and set has the same edge as a shooter who just passes the first test with 482 on-axis throws. The rest of the results are better than the 482 on-axis shooter but significantly worse than the 482 on-axis shooter who passed all three SmartCraps tests—even if he just barely passed them.

Recommendation for Good On-Axis Results with Random Pitch and Random Double Pitches: *Use the 3V set and Place bet the 6. Do not use the Hardway set and do not make any Hop bets, as the house has an edge on all these bets.*

More Simulations:

Three more sets of 1,000-roll simulations were run, and the results are recapped below followed by comments for each set of simulations.

Simulation A: 500 On Axis, 150 Primaries, and 100 Double-Pitch 7s
(This shooter passes all three tests with a better on-axis score of 50 percent.)

Hardway Set Results:
Placing the 6 has a *player edge* of about 8.3 percent.
Hopping the 3:3 has a *player edge* of about 16.3 percent.

3V Set Results:
Placing the 6 has a *player edge* of about 10.6 percent.
Hopping the 3:3 has a *player edge* of about 16.4 percent.

This controlled thrower has even more of an advantage over the house than the dice controller who barely passed all three SmartCraps tests. Since the performance of this on-axis dice controller is better than the performance of the 482/144/98 shooter in all categories, it makes sense that the edges will be higher also.

Simulation A Recommendations: *If you are strictly going after Hop bets and not placing the 6, then you can use either the Hardway or the 3V since the difference is marginal. However, if you also want to place the 6, then the 3V set is the preferred set since you have a much greater edge over the house doing do.*

Simulation B: 600 On Axis, 150 Primaries (Random), 150 Double-Pitch 7s (Random)
(*This shooter has a full 60 percent of his shots on axis. This amounts to a 25 percent improvement over the 482 on-axis shooter who just passes*

the first SmartCraps test. The other two SmartCraps tests merely indicate random results.)

Hardway Set Results:
Placing the 6 has a *house edge* of about 3.5 percent.
Hopping the 3:3 has a *player edge* of about 16.4 percent.

3V Set Results:
Placing the 6 has a *player edge* of about 7.3 percent.
Hopping the 3:3 has a *player edge* of about 16 percent.

Most of the results here make sense. The 60 percent on-axis controlled shooter has an improved edge over the 50 percent on-axis shooter if we use random results for the other two SmartCraps tests (Tests 2 and 3). This occurs on all simulations except placing the 6 using the Hardway set, where the house edge becomes a whopping 3.5 percent in contrast to the 2.4 percent house edge of the 50 percent on-axis shooter.

> **Simulation B Recommendations:** *Use the 3V to place and hop your 6 bets. You have a slightly smaller edge over the house with the 3V on Hop bets but a much larger edge over the Place bet of the 6.*

Simulation C: 600 On Axis, 176 Primaries, 125 Double-Pitch 7s
(This shooter has the same 600 on-axis rolls but also passes Tests 2 and 3, which are the primary and double-pitch-7 tests. This is an advanced shooter.)

Hardway Set Results:
Placing the 6 has a *player edge* of about 6.3 percent.
Hopping the 3:3 has a *player edge* of about 36.4 percent

3V Set Results:
Placing the 6 has a *player edge* of about 16.3 percent.
Hopping the 3:3 has a *player edge* of about 36.4 percent.

All edges in this simulation are for the player, with the 3V set greatly outperforming the Hardway set on the placing of the 6. This makes sense, as it is the preferred set for hitting the 6.

The more interesting result is that the set used (be it Hardway or 3V) makes little difference when betting the hopping 3:3. At each level of on-axis control, the edge for hopping the 3:3 is almost identical for both the Hardway and 3V sets.

> **Simulation C Recommendation:** *You should use the 3V if you fall into this category. The Place bet on the 6 is much more powerful than on the Hardway set, while Hop betting for both sets remains the same.*

Our other common measure of dice control—the SRR—does not measure on-axis control; it simply measures the number of 7s versus the other numbers. By reducing the number of 7s that appear, the player's advantage is increased. Unlike the SmartCraps measurement of on-axis control that can be proved in as few as 100 to 200 rolls, it takes 5,000 or more rolls to establish a viable SRR.

Let's take a look at what kind of advantage different SRR levels produce when placing the 6 and when hopping the 3:3.

Because SRR simply measures the appearance of 7s relative to other numbers, the dice set is irrelevant. Any dice set the SRR shooter uses to produce the stated SRR will produce the same results because all the other numbers have to be considered to appear in a random fashion, as I stated earlier (this is a rule of thumb as opposed to a real rule of nature); only the 7s are reduced. Though the edges could be calculated strictly by math, SmartCraps was used to run simulations to get the resulting edges.

For the purposes of comparison, four different SRRs were used: 1:6.5, 1:7.0, 1:7.5, and 1:8. For reference, an SRR of 1:6.3 can overcome the edge of only the lowest-house-edge bets in craps. The excellent SRR of 8.0 is extremely hard to obtain. Only top-notch controllers will achieve this level of performance. The set being used throughout is the Hardway set. In the following examples I talk about the 6, but all the information relates to the 8 as well.

Placing the 6 (Random House Edge Is 1.52 Percent)

SRR	6.5	7.0	7.5	8.0
Player's Edge	3.59%	8.28%	12.57%	16.58%
Difference from Random	+5.11	+9.80	+14.09	+18.10

Hopping the 3:3 (Random House Edge Is 13.89 Percent)

SRR	6.5	7.0	7.5	8.0
Player's Edge	-12.70%	-11.49%	-10.48%	-9.59%
Difference from Random	+1.19	+2.40	+3.41	+4.30

Notice that the player's edge for placing the 6 rises dramatically as the SRR increases. An SRR of 7.0 has roughly the same player edge as an on-axis controller who gets 600 on axis, 176 primaries, and 125 double-pitch 7s out of 1,000 rolls. The interesting numbers are those for the hopping of the 3:3. As the SRR increases, the edge improves only slightly. Even at a whopping 8.0 SRR, the house edge on those Hop bets is still almost 10 percent! Clearly, if SRR is your only measurement, stick with placing the 6 and forget about hopping the 3:3.

> **Recommendations for SRR Betting:** *You should avoid all Hop bets, as these still carry hugely high house edges against you. Concentrate on the traditional betting regimens of the game even with a large SRR. Without on-axis control, the traditional betting methods are by far the best.*

Conclusions

Placing the 6 is not always the best bet. Better on-axis control will tilt the result in favor of betting a Hop bet. However, better on-axis control only is not as powerful as one might think. In fact, if on-axis control is the only modification in evidence, certain results get worse—for example, placing the 6 using the Hardway set with random primary and double-pitch-7 results (SmartCraps Tests 2 and 3). In fact the better the on-axis control without passing Tests 2 and 3 in SmartCraps, the worse the results on placing the 6 while using the Hardway set.

In order to get maximum results, *passing all three SmartCraps tests is mandatory*. As an example, passing all three tests with 1,000 rolls of 500 on axis (50 percent), 150 primaries, and 100 double pitches will produce more profit for you than 1,000 rolls with 600 on axis, 125 primaries (random result), and 125 double pitches (random result).

The more on-axis throws you have, the more the set you use matters. The more on-axis throws, the better the Hop bets look. A Hop bet could be better than placing the 6 with an on-axis-throw rate of as little as 48.2 percent (482 primary hits in 1,000 throws). Remember 44.4 percent would be random results, showing no axis control.

CHAPTER 4

The Hardway Set Anomaly

As mentioned in Chapter 3, using the Hardway set while placing the 6 (or 8) can actually hurt the on-axis dice controller. The table below summarizes the results of several different dice-control levels. All of the On-Axises, Primaries, and Double-Pitch 7s are based on 1,000 rolls of the dice to make it easier to reflect all the data.

SmartCraps Results—Player Edge Placing the 6—Hardway Set

On-Axis*	Random	482	482	500	500	600	600
Primaries*		121	144	125	150	150	176
Double-Pitch 7s*		121	98	125	100	150	125
Calculated (Random)	-1.52%	-1.52%	-1.52%	-1.52%	-1.52%	-1.52%	-1.52%
Player Edge from Sim	-1.52%	**-2.30%**	+7.60%	**-2.42%**	+8.30%	**-3.49%**	+6.33%
Difference	0.00%	**-0.78%**	+9.12%	**-0.90%**	+9.82%	**-1.97%**	+7.85%

*Number of rolls out of 1,000-roll sample.

The bold cells indicate results that on the surface seem wrong based on our traditional view of craps betting. How can using the Hardway set—a set that is *the best* at avoiding the 7—produce results that are worse than normal distribution percentages (again, some would call this "worse than random" or "reverse control" results) when the shooter exhibits on-axis control? Surely this has to be a bug in the software, right?

Notice, however, that this phenomenon only occurs when there is on-axis control without any pitch control. Pitch refers to the up-and-down motion of the rotation. When an airplane pitches up, its nose raises; when it pitches down, its nose drops. Pitch control means keeping each die spinning at the same speed as the other. In each instance where results are "worse" than normal random distribution, the pitch control is nonexistent—the Primaries and Double-Pitch 7s are merely random.

To prove that the seemingly impossible results make sense, we have to consider what happens when we exert on-axis control of the dice.

The Hardway set places the 1s and 6s on the axis through the dice. This means that the more on-axis control there is, the fewer percent of the time a 1-pip or 6-pip will appear. *Perfect* on-axis control would result in *no* 1s or 6s ever showing. Reducing the appearance of 1s and 6s will alter the distribution of numbers thrown.

Let's look at what happens with a perfect on-axis dice controller. No 1s or 6s will appear. Since no 1s or 6s appear, there will never be a 2, 3, 11, or 12 result. By eliminating the 1 and 6 from play, there are now only 16 possible result combinations—not the 36 possible result combinations when all numbers are in play.

Here are the distributions for a random shooter versus a perfect on-axis controller without pitch control.

Result	2	3	4	5	6	7	8	9	10	11	12
Random	1	2	3	4	5	6	5	4	3	2	1
100% On Axis			1	2	3	4	3	2	1		

You can clearly see what is happening. In a random game where all numbers are in play, there are five ways to make a 6 and six ways to make a 7. The house pays 7-to-6 for a 1.52 percent house edge. When the 1-pip and 6-pip are out of play but the results are still random, there are three ways to make the number 6 and four ways to make a 7. The house still pays 7-to-6 for a high house edge of 7.14 percent.

So, using the Hardway set, the better on-axis control a shooter has *without any pitch control* will cause him to do poorer with Place bets. The previous simulation results track well with the above numbers. For a random shooter 444 (44.4 percent) out of 1,000 rolls will be on axis. This results in a 1.52 percent house edge when placing the number 6. The simulations show a house edge of 2.30 percent with 482 (48.2 percent) out of 1,000 rolls on axis, a 2.42 percent house edge with 500 (50 percent) out of 1,000 rolls on axis, and 3.49 percent house edge with 600 (60 percent) out of 1,000 rolls on axis.

Clearly, on-axis control is only a part of the necessary equation resulting in profits at the craps table. The dice set that is used takes an increasingly more important role as on-axis proficiency increases. On-axis control must be combined with pitch-control proficiency and the proper dice set to maximize a controlled shooter's profits.

With so many different things to look at, how can you find out where you stand with dice control? SmartCraps is the only software program I am aware of that has *all* the information shooters need to cash in on their specific level of dice-control skill. It will tell you exactly your degree of on-axis control (if any) and show you the best sets and the associated edges for any bets at the craps table. If you intend to be serious about getting an on-axis edge at craps, SmartCraps is essential. Get it and use it.

CHAPTER 5
Looking at Other Hop Bets

We have seen how various levels of on-axis dice control and SRR performance affect the player's edge when placing the number 6 and hopping the 3:3. Now let's look at some other typically bad bets. For the remaining bets, only the Hardway set and the SmartCraps-recommended set will be used for on-axis control simulations.

For the following tables, dice sets are described by their faces. T=Top Face; F=Face to the Player. Since there are two dice, each die's set will be given to you.

Here we go.

Hop 2:4 Bets (Random House Edge Is 11.11 Percent)

The results are summarized in the tables below.

The Hardway Set: Random Pitch Control

On Axis	482	500	600
Primary Hits	121	125	150
Double Pitches	121	125	150
Player's Edge	-4.08%	-0.22%	19.91%
Difference from Random	+7.03	+10.89	+31.02

The Hardway Set: Minimal Passing Pitch Control

On Axis	482	500	600
Primary Hits	144	150	176
Double Pitches	98	100	125
Player's Edge	-4.05%	0.17%	19.52%
Difference from Random	+7.06	+11.28	+30.63

SmartCraps Set (T2F4:T4F2): Random Pitch Control (T2F4:T4F2)

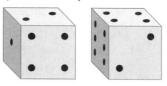

On Axis	482	500	600
Primary Hits	121	125	150
Double Pitches	121	125	150
Player's Edge	-3.35%	-0.20%	19.91%
Difference from Random	+7.76	+10.91	+31.02

SmartCraps Set (T2F4:T4F2): Minimal Passing Pitch Control (T2F4:T4F2)

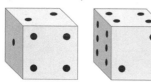

On Axis	482	500	600
Primary Hits	144	150	176
Double Pitches	98	100	125
Player's Edge	14.99%	19.76%	40.75%
Difference from Random	+26.10	+30.87	+51.86

SRR	6.5	7.0	7.5	8.0
Player's Edge	-9.81%	-8.70%	-7.68%	-6.72%
Difference from Random	+1.30	+2.41	+3.43	+4.39

All of the on-axis percentages and SRR percentages closely follow the edges for hopping the 3:3. The actual percentage edge for hopping 2:4 is higher than for hopping the 3:3, but the difference from random is almost identical whether using the Hardway set or the SmartCraps-recommended set. All of the same recommendations for hopping the 3:3 would also apply to hopping 2:4. In fact, with good on-axis and pitch control, it is preferable to hop the 2:4 because the initial house edge is lower, giving a higher player edge to the on-axis shooter.

Hop 1:5 Bets (Random House Edge Is 11.11 Percent)

The results are summarized in the tables below.

The Hardway Set: Random Pitch Control

On Axis	482	500	600
Primary Hits	121	125	150
Double Pitches	121	125	150
Player's Edge	-17.18%	-20.07%	-36.00%
Difference from Random	-6.07	-8.96	-24.89

The Hardway Set: Minimal Passing Pitch Control

On Axis	482	500	600
Primary Hits	144	150	176
Double Pitches	98	100	125
Player's Edge	-17.11%	-20.06%	-39.95%
Difference from Random	-6.00	-8.95	-28.84

SmartCraps Set (T1F5:T5F1): Random Pitch Control (T1F5:T5F1)

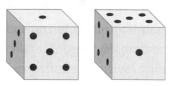

On Axis	482	500	600
Primary Hits	121	125	150
Double Pitches	121	125	150
Player's Edge	-3.14%	0.14%	19.98%
Difference from Random	+7.97	+11.25	+31.09

SmartCraps Set (T1F5:T5F1): Minimal Passing Pitch Control (T1F5:T5F1)

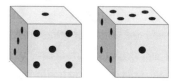

On Axis	482	500	600
Primary Hits	144	150	176
Double Pitches	98	100	125
Player's Edge	15.05%	20.16%	40.75%
Difference from Random	+26.16	+31.27	+51.86

SRR	6.5	7.0	7.5	8.0
Player's Edge	-9.86%	-8.71%	-7.72%	-6.90%
Difference from Random	+1.25	+2.40	+3.39	+4.21

The Hardway set results deteriorate with improved on-axis control. This is because the 1-pip is required to win this bet. With better on-axis control, fewer 1s appear. When using the SmartCraps recommended set, the results mirror the hopping 2:4 bet results. The same is true for the SRR results.

As stated many times, random levels of on-axis performance that have a good SRR will also allow the controlled shooter to get an edge over the casino, but that edge is not as powerful as those on-axis shooters who have strong performances, as previously shown.

Some More Radical Betting Options

Hardway Bets

Included among the worst wagers on a craps table are the Hardway bets. The house edge for a random shooter is 9.09 percent for the hard 6 or 8 and 11.11 percent for the hard 4 or 10. Ordinarily these are bets to avoid like the bubonic plague. Still can on-axis controlled shooters turn the tables on these bets like they can with the individual Hop bets?

Let's look at the same levels of on-axis and pitch control and the same SRR performance levels. Simulations for all these performance levels using the Hardway set and the SmartCraps-recommended set were run for the hard 6 and 8 and hard 4 and 10. Simulations for the four SRR levels previously used were also run.

Hard 6 and 8 (Random House Edge Is 9.09 Percent)

Hardway Set: Random Pitch Control

On Axis	482	500	600
Primary Hits	121	125	150
Double Pitches	121	125	150
Player's Edge	-3.83%	-1.70%	9.66%
Difference from Random	+5.26	+7.39	+18.75

Hardway Set: Minimal Passing Pitch Control

On Axis	482	500	600
Primary Hits	144	150	176
Double Pitches	98	100	125
Player's Edge	21.27%	25.15%	36.05%
Difference from Random	+30.36	+34.24	+45.14

SmartCraps Set 3V (T3F5:T3F1): Random Pitch Control (T3F5:T3F1)

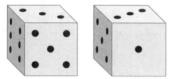

On Axis	482	500	600
Primary Hits	121	125	150
Double Pitches	121	125	150
Player's Edge	-1.14%	1.99%	21.85%
Difference from Random	+7.95	+11.08	+30.94

SmartCraps Set 3V (T3F5:T3F1): Minimal Passing Pitch Control (T3F5:T3F1)

On Axis	482	500	600
Primary Hits	144	150	176
Double Pitches	98	100	125
Player's Edge	17.59%	22.53%	42.81%
Difference from Random	+26.68	+31.62	+51.90

SRR	6.5	7.0	7.5	8.0
Player's Edge	-4.37%	0.02%	4.02%	7.69%
Difference from Random	+4.72	+9.11	+13.11	+16.78

For hard 6 and hard 8 bets, both the Hardway set and the 3V set perform very well. The Hardway set actually performs better than the 3V except at the top control level simulated. A minimally passing on-axis and pitch-controlled shooter has a 30 percent swing in edge—from a 9.09

percent house edge to a whopping 21.27 percent player edge. The results clearly show that a moderately on-axis and pitch-controlled shooter will fare much better with Hardway bets on the 6 and 8 than placing these numbers. The same cannot be said for the SRR results.

Hard 4 and 10 (Random House Edge Is 11.11 Percent)

SmartCraps Set Is Hardway Set: Random Pitch Control

On Axis	482	500	600
Primary Hits	121	125	150
Double Pitches	121	125	150
Player's Edge	-5.52%	-2.44%	11.94%
Difference from Random	+5.89	+8.67	+23.05

SmartCraps Set Is Hardway Set: Minimal Passing Pitch Control

On Axis	482	500	600
Primary Hits	144	150	176
Double Pitches	98	100	125
Player's Edge	21.15%	26.10%	41.34%
Difference from Random	+32.26	+37.21	+52.45

SRR	6.5	7.0	7.5	8.0
Player's Edge	-5.52%	-0.06%	4.95%	9.64%
Difference from Random	+5.59	+11.05	+16.06	+20.75

For hard 4 and hard 10 bets, the Hardway set is the preferred set. It performs admirably when coupled with pitch control. Even a minimally passing score on all three SmartCraps tests overcomes the 11.11 percent house edge and gives the player a better than 21 percent edge—a 32 percent swing! This is dramatically better than placing the 6 with the same level of control. The SRR numbers are nowhere near the on-axis-control numbers.

Hopping 7 Bets (Random House Edge Is 11.11 Percent)

Let's look at what happens if we bet hopping 7s. This means we are betting a multiple of $3 on any combination of dice that total a 7. These are 1:6 and 6:1, 2:5 and 5:2, and 3:4 and 4:3. If a 7 appears, only one of the three bets will win, and the others will lose. If no 7 appears on the roll, all three bets lose. The results are summarized in the tables below.

Hardway Set: Random Pitch Control

On Axis	482	500	600
Primary Hits	121	125	150
Double Pitches	121	125	150
Player's Edge	-7.72%	-6.60%	1.30%
Difference from Random	+3.39	+4.51	+12.41

Hardway Set: Minimal Passing Pitch Control

On Axis	482	500	600
Primary Hits	144	150	176
Double Pitches	98	100	125
Player's Edge	-20.04%	-19.95%	-12.10%
Difference from Random	-8.93	-8.84	-0.99

SmartCraps Set (T2F4:T5F3—All 7s): Random Pitch Control (T2F4:T5F3—All 7s)

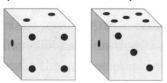

On Axis	482	500	600
Primary Hits	121	125	150
Double Pitches	121	125	150
Player's Edge	-7.72%	-6.60%	1.30%
Difference from Random	+3.39	+4.51	+12.41

SmartCraps Set (T2F4:T5F3—All-Sevens): Minimal Passing Pitch Control
(T2F4:T5F3—All-Sevens)

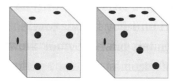

On Axis	482	500	600
Primary Hits	144	150	176
Double Pitches	98	100	125
Player's Edge	4.42%	6.74%	15.11%
Difference from Random	+15.53	+17.85	+26.22

SRR	6.5	5.5	5.0
Player's Edge	-17.95%	-2.99%	6.72%
Difference from Random	-6.84	+8.12	ı 17.83

The most interesting results above are those for random pitch control. It doesn't matter if the Hardway set or the All 7s set is used. The same results occur. All that matters is the level of on-axis control the shooter has. For example, with 482 on-axis rolls out of 1,000 rolls, the player's edge is -7.72 percent with either the Hardway or the All 7s set. Also, as on-axis performance improves without pitch control, the results improve with the Hardway set—something that is counterintuitive. The Hardway set is supposed to reduce the appearance of the 7. The strange performance occurs for the same reason that performance declines when placing the 6. As the shooter becomes better at reducing the appearance of the 1s and 6s, the 7 becomes much more powerful.

For the on-axis controllers with minimally passing pitch control, the results—as expected—are "worse" than random. The results steadily improve using the All 7s set. However, even though the house edge is the same as hopping the 6s, the results are not as good. This is most likely because we are betting on the 1:6 and 6:1 even though this combination appears less frequently with good on-axis control. To prove this,

I ran a simulation where the only hopping 7 bets were the 2:5 and 5:2 and the 3:4 and 4:3. The results of the simulation were identical to the Hop 2:4 and Hop 5:1 using the SmartCraps recommended sets. So, with proper betting, a proficient on-axis controller could make just as much on hopping the 7s as hopping the 1:5 and 2:4.

Whirl Bets (Random House Edge Is 13.33 Percent)

The Whirl bet has one of the highest house edges of all the craps bets—13.33 percent. In essence the Whirl (sometimes called "World") is a bet on any non-point number. It is a one-roll bet on the 2, 3, 11, 12, and 7, so it is actually five different one-roll bets. If you win one of them, you lose the other four—or you lose all five if the other non-Whirl numbers show. The winning numbers are paid at different rates—2 and 12 have a house edge of 13.89 percent; 3 and 11 have a house edge of 11.11 percent; and the 7 has a house edge of a monstrous 16.67 percent.

Simulations were run using all the same on-axis, pitch, and SRR combinations that were used in previous examples. The results are summarized in the tables below.

Hardway Set: Random Pitch Control

On Axis	482	500	600
Primary Hits	121	125	150
Double Pitches	121	125	150
Player's Edge	-17.39%	-19.50%	-30.57%
Difference from Random	-4.06	-6.17	-17.24

Hardway Set: Minimal Passing Pitch Control

On Axis	482	500	600
Primary Hits	144	150	176
Double Pitches	98	100	125
Player's Edge	-19.68%	-21.95%	-33.06%
Difference from Random	-6.35	-8.62	-19.73

SmartCraps Set (T1F5:T2F6): Random Pitch Control (T1F5:T2F6)

On Axis	482	500	600
Primary Hits	121	125	150
Double Pitches	121	125	150
Player's Edge	-6.90%	-3.75%	13.54%
Difference from Random	+6.43	+9.58	+26.87

SmartCraps Set (T1F5:T2F6): Random Pitch Control (T1F5:T2F6)

On Axis	482	500	600
Primary Hits	144	150	176
Double Pitches	98	100	125
Player's Edge	0.42%	4.28%	21.71%
Difference from Random	+13.75	+17.61	+35.04

SRR	6.5	7.0	7.5	8.0
Player's Edge	-13.46%	-13.68%	13.84%	-13.97%
Difference from Random	-0.13	-0.35	-0.51	-0.64

Since the Hardway set has the 1 and 6 on the axis, as the shooter obtains better on-axis performance, fewer 1s and 6s appear. When fewer 1-pips and 6-pips appear, fewer 2s, 3s, 11s, and 12s appear. The Hardway set also reduces the appearance of the 7, so fewer 7s appear as the on-axis controller's prowess grows. This means that the better you are at on-axis control, the worse you will do betting the Whirl. The numbers just shown corroborate this.

If the SmartCraps-recommended set is used, a decent player edge can be developed. The results are nowhere near those for hopping the 2:4 or 1:5, however. Looking at the SRR results, they are bad and don't improve as the SRR improves.

The Whirl bet should be avoided no matter how good a dice controller you become.

Horn Bets (Random House Edge Is 12.50 Percent)

The Horn bet is a Whirl bet without the 7 included. It is a one-roll bet on a 2, 3, 11, or 12. It is usually bet in multiples of four, as it is really four individual bets. If you win one of the bets, you lose the other three; otherwise you lose all four when non-Horn numbers appear. Because the highest house edge of 16.67 percent on the 7 is not a part of the Horn bet, the combined house edge is better for the player than the Whirl bet.

Simulations were run using all the same on-axis, pitch, and SRR combinations that were used in previous examples. The results are summarized in the tables below.

Hardway Set: Random Pitch Control

On Axis	482	500	600
Primary Hits	121	125	150
Double Pitches	121	125	150
Player's Edge	-18.38%	-21.27%	-36.94%
Difference from Random	-5.88	-8.77	-24.44

Hardway Set: Minimal Passing Pitch Control

On Axis	482	500	600
Primary Hits	144	150	176
Double Pitches	98	100	125
Player's Edge	-18.34%	-21.18%	-36.92%
Difference from Random	-5.84	-8.68	-24.42

SmartCraps Set (T1F5:T2F6): Random Pitch Control (T1F5:T2F6)

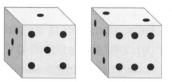

On Axis	482	500	600
Primary Hits	121	125	150
Double Pitches	121	125	150
Player's Edge	5.08%	-1.56%	18.18%
Difference from Random	+17.58	+10.94	+30.68

SmartCraps Set (T1F5:T2F6): Minimal Passing Pitch Control (T1F5:T2F6)

On Axis	482	500	600
Primary Hits	144	150	176
Double Pitches	98	100	125
Player's Edge	4.05%	8.49%	28.45%
Difference from Random	+16.55	+20.99	+40.95

SRR	6.5	7.0	7.5	8.0
Player's Edge	-11.05%	-9.95%	-8.96%	-8.09%
Difference from Random	+1.45	+2.55	+3.54	+4.41

Since the Hardway set has the 1-pips and 6-pips on the axis, as the shooter obtains better on-axis performance, fewer 1-pips and 6-pips appear. When fewer 1s and 6s appear, the fewer the numbers 2, 3, 11, and 12 appear. This means that the better you are at on-axis control, the worse you will do betting the Horn using the Hardway set. The numbers just shown corroborate this.

If the SmartCraps-recommended set is used, a decent player edge can be developed. The results are nowhere near those for hopping the 2:4 or 1:5, however. Looking at the SRR results, they are bad but improve somewhat as the SRR improves.

The results for the Horn bet are generally better than for the Whirl bet. This is because the 7 and its associated house edge of 16.67 percent are not included in the mix. As with the Whirl bet, it is a good idea to avoid the Horn bet. You will make more money on the 6 or 8.

Crapless Craps

So far we have looked at a variety of normally horrendous bets. Some of them remain terrible bets, but others become more lucrative for the on-axis dice controller than normally good bets.

Crapless craps (or "never-ever craps") is a derivative of traditional craps where the player never has to worry about losing a Pass Line bet to a craps number (2, 3, or 12) on the come-out roll. In crapless craps all numbers other than the 7 become point numbers if they are rolled on the come-out. While seemingly a good thing, this game tilts the house edge for Pass and Come bets further to the house because the 11, which is a winner on the come-out in standard craps, also becomes a point when rolled in crapless craps. That is not good for the random rollers.

There are still great opportunities for on-axis dice controllers in crapless craps. All Place, Buy, and Hop bets have the same returns as the standard game, so hopping the 3:3, 2:4, or 1:5 offers the same money-making opportunities. In crapless craps, however, there is the opportunity to *buy* the 2, 3, 11, and 12. Many casinos that offer crapless craps allow a buy on these numbers for as little as $10 and charge a $1 commission up to a $25 bet. True odds on making the 3 or 11 are 3-to-1. True odds for making the 2 or 12 are 6-to-1. In casinos that only collect the commission on wins, the house edges for buying these numbers is as follows:

- Buying the 3 or 11 for $10 with $1 vig on wins only has a 2.50 percent house edge; the 2 or 12 has a 1.43 percent house edge.

- Buying the 3 or 11 for $25 with $1 vig on wins only has a 1 percent house edge; the 2 or 12 has a 0.57 percent house edge.

These are great bets—especially at the $25 level—rivaling the best bets in the traditional game.

So let's take a look at what controlled shooters can expect at crapless craps. Simulations were run using all the same on-axis, pitch, and SRR combinations that were used in the previous examples.

Buying the 3 or 11
Buy for $10 with $1 Commission (Vig) on Wins Only
(Random House Edge Is 2.50 Percent)

Hardway Set: Random Pitch Control

On Axis	482	500	600
Primary Hits	121	125	150
Double Pitches	121	125	150
Player's Edge	-10.01%	-13.14%	-31.57%
Difference from Random	-7.51	-10.64	-29.07

Hardway Set: Minimal Passing Pitch Control

On-Axis	482	500	600
Primary Hits	144	150	176
Double Pitches	98	100	125
Player's Edge	0.11%	-2.56%	-23.34%
Difference from Random	+2.61	-0.06	-20.84

Clearly, the Hardway set is not the way to go. In all but one instance the results are worse than random.

SmartCraps Set (T1F5:T2F6): Random Pitch Control (T1F5:T2F6)

On Axis	482	500	600
Primary Hits	121	125	150
Double Pitches	121	125	150
Player's Edge	1.55%	2.56%	10.21%
Difference from Random	+4.05	+5.06	+12.71

SmartCraps Set (T1F5:T2F6): Minimal Passing Pitch Control (T1F5:T2F6)

On Axis	482	500	600
Primary Hits	144	150	176
Double Pitches	98	100	125
Player's Edge	14.64%	16.59%	23.08%
Difference from Random	+17.14	+19.09	+25.58

Using the SmartCraps-recommended set dramatically improves the results. However, hopping the 6s is still a better strategy.

SRR	6.5	7.0	7.5	8.0
Player's Edge	4.55%	11.11%	17.41%	23.32%
Difference from Random	+7.05	+13.61	+19.91	+25.82

Improved SRRs have a dramatic effect on payback. In fact this is the best SRR performance of any bet we have examined. But it is still not as good as hopping the 6 with good on-axis and passing pitch control.

Buy for $25 With $1 Vig on Wins Only (Random House Edge Is 1.00 Percent)

Hardway Set: Random Pitch Control

On Axis	482	500	600
Primary Hits	121	125	150
Double Pitches	121	125	150
Player's Edge	-8.78%	-12.00%	-30.86%
Difference from Random	-7.78	-11.00	-29.00

Hardway Set: Minimal Passing Pitch Control

On Axis	482	500	600
Primary Hits	144	150	176
Double Pitches	98	100	125
Player's Edge	1.64%	-1.12%	-22.45%
Difference from Random	+2.64	-0.12	-21.45

Again, the Hardway set is not the way to go. In all but one instance the results are worse than random.

SmartCraps Set (T1F5:T2F6): Random Pitch Control (T1F5:T2F6)

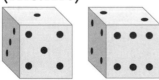

On Axis	482	500	600
Primary Hits	121	125	150
Double Pitches	121	125	150
Player's Edge	3.12%	4.16%	12.06%
Difference from Random	+4.12	+5.16	+13.06

SmartCraps Set (T1F5:T2F6): Minimal Passing Pitch Control (T1F5:T2F6)

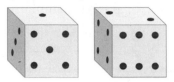

On Axis	482	500	600
Primary Hits	144	150	176
Double Pitches	98	100	125
Player's Edge	16.65%	18.67%	25.39%
Difference from Random	+17.65	+19.67	+26.39

Again, using the SmartCraps-recommended set dramatically improves the results, but again, hopping 6s is still the better strategy.

SRR	6.5	7.0	7.5	8.0
Player's Edge	6.22%	12.99%	19.51%	25.64%
Difference from Random	+7.22	+13.99	+20.51	+26.64

As with the $10 buy of the 3 or 11, improved SRRs have a dramatic effect on payback. In fact, this is the best SRR performance of any bet we have examined. It is still not as good as a hopping 6 with good on-axis and passing pitch control.

Buying the 2 or 12
Buy for $10 With $1 Vig on Wins Only
(Random House Edge Is 1.43 Percent)

Hardway Set: Random Pitch Control

On Axis	482	500	600
Primary Hits	121	125	150
Double Pitches	121	125	150
Player's Edge	-9.88%	-13.58%	-33.91%
Difference from Random	-8.45	-12.15	-32.48

Hardway Set: Minimal Passing Pitch Control

On Axis	482	500	600
Primary Hits	144	150	176
Double Pitches	98	100	125
Player's Edge	-1.89%	-1.23%	-24.98%
Difference from Random	-0.46	+0.20	-23.55

As with all of the crapless craps bets examined, the Hardway set is not the way to go. In all but one instance the results are worse than random.

SmartCraps Set (T1F5:T1F5): Random Pitch Control (T1F5:T1F5)

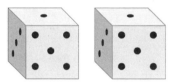

On Axis	482	500	600
Primary Hits	121	125	150
Double Pitches	121	125	150
Player's Edge	2.79%	4.52%	13.41%
Difference from Random	+4.22	+5.95	+14.84

SmartCraps Set (T1F5:T1F5): Minimal Passing Pitch Control (T1F5:T1F5)

On Axis	482	500	600
Primary Hits	144	150	176
Double Pitches	98	100	125
Player's Edge	33.12%	37.24%	44.42%
Difference from Random	+34.55	+33.09	+45.85

Using the SmartCraps-recommended set dramatically improves the results. These results are now the best of any bet we have explored so far!

SRR	6.5	7.0	7.5	8.0
Player's Edge	6.92%	14.83%	22.54%	30.06%
Difference from Random	+8.35	+16.26	+23.97	+31.49

Improved SRRs have a dramatic effect on payback. This is the best SRR performance of any bet we have examined. It is still not as good as hopping the 6 or buying the 2 or 12 with good on-axis and passing pitch control, however.

Buy for $25 With $1 Vig on Wins Only (Random House Edge Is 0.57 Percent)

Hardway Set: Random Pitch Control

On Axis	482	500	600
Primary Hits	121	125	150
Double Pitches	121	125	150
Player's Edge	-9.18%	-12.93%	-33.53%
Difference from Random	-8.61	-12.36	-32.96

Hardway Set: Minimal Passing Pitch Control

On Axis	482	500	600
Primary Hits	144	150	176
Double Pitches	98	100	125
Player's Edge	2.78%	0.38%	-24.49%
Difference from Random	+3.35	+0.19	-23.92

Forget about the Hardway set. It is not the way to go. In all but two instances the results are worse than random.

SmartCraps Set (T1F5:T1F5): Random Pitch Control (T1F5:T1F5)

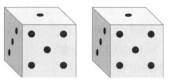

On Axis	482	500	600
Primary Hits	121	125	150
Double Pitches	121	125	150
Player's Edge	3.71%	5.46%	14.52%
Difference from Random	+4.28	+6.03	+15.09

SmartCraps Set (T1F5:T1F5): Minimal Passing Pitch Control (T1F5:T1F5)

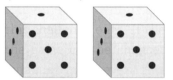

On Axis	482	500	600
Primary Hits	144	150	176
Double Pitches	98	100	125
Player's Edge	34.66%	38.87%	46.23%
Difference from Random	+35.23	+39.44	+46.80

Wow! Look at those numbers! Even with minimal passing grades on all three SmartCraps tests, the on-axis controlled shooter has almost a 35 percent edge over the house. That means the potential to make $35 for every $100 wagered. If you are an on-axis controlled shooter and can find this bet, you can become very rich indeed.

SRR	6.5	7.0	7.5	8.0
Player's Edge	7.91%	15.97%	23.84%	31.53%
Difference from Random	+8.48	+16.54	+24.41	+32.10

As with all of the crapless bets examined, improved SRRs have a dramatic effect on payback. This is, in fact, now the best SRR performance of any bet we have examined. It is still not as good as hopping the 6 or buying the 2 or 12 with good on-axis and passing pitch control.

Conclusions

Throughout this chapter we have examined wagers that might ordinarily be considered bad to horrifying. We have seen how on-axis dice control can turn conventional wisdom on its head. With good on-axis control, hopping the 6 becomes a significantly better bet than placing the 6. Using the Hardway set—the set that best protects against the 7—can actually reduce your edge to make it worse than random with on-axis dice control that *lacks* pitch control.

While there are dramatic changes to some conventional wisdom, other pieces hold true. Whirl and Horn bets, with their initial high house edges and combinations of numbers required to win, are very difficult to beat. There is just too much working against you. With the proper dice set and a high degree of skill you can get around a 20 percent edge, but with the same level of skill, the proper dice set, and the proper choice of bets, you can achieve nearly a 50 percent edge over the house! Yes, if you really get into the realm of the elite, there is a fortune to be made at craps.

The keys are practice, discipline, and knowledge. To develop any physical skill, practice and discipline are always required. In craps, you must also have the proper knowledge—knowledge this book offers to you, knowledge of your own individual skill level, and knowledge of the best dice sets and bets for your skill level.

While the SRR can give you an appreciation that you are controlling the dice, it cannot tell you the best sets or bets. For that you need a tool such as SmartCraps. While it may have been possible to gain the information presented in this chapter from pure math, SmartCraps made it easy to understand, which is necessary to make the practice and discipline pay the biggest dividends.

Using Radical Betting in Your Game Plan

My recommendation on radical betting is simple: pass all three SmartCraps tests before you try to incorporate Hop betting into your game plan. Hop betting could be very dangerous if you are overrating your skill, which many dice controllers unfortunately do. If SmartCraps shows that you are a marginal on-axis player, your skill level will go up and down. If you have slightly more downs, you might find that consistently losing money on those Hop bets will make you shoot worse than you would normally shoot because you will probably get emotionally uptight. An uptight dice controller becomes a poorer dice controller.

So I am not going to recommend abandoning the placing of 6 and 8 or the buying of the 4 or 10 with the commission paid on the win only. We still have player edges on these bets when using the 3V or 2V sets. Even Dominator and Stickman and other elite shooters back up their Hop bets with these safer bets. In fact, most of the elite shooters will bet more on the traditional bets, perhaps as a remnant of their savvy craps play in the days when they were novice dice controllers.

Yes, the true mathematical way to play is for you to abandon the Place bets and just go all out on the Hop bets if you are an advanced on-axis shooter. That sounds good, but I know very few who can do that without getting a little uptight. It is a giant step from normal advantage play to make such a move. If you think you can do that, fine; but I think most of the world's advanced shooters will find that a combination of Place and Hop bets would be better for their shooting and for their emotional well-being.

Passing all three SmartCraps tests—the higher the scores on each, the better for radical play—will allow you to have confidence in adding radical forms of betting to your arsenal. You should practice your radical Hop betting at home for thousands of rolls before you ever attempt such a betting method in the casino. Even though our simulations used 1,000 rolls as a theoretical norm, you should roll far more to get a true sense of what you can do in this area of radical play.

A *Strong* Word of Caution

I wrote it earlier: "There is a fortune to be made at craps." Now, let me bring you down to earth a little. Dominator and I have learned from the bitter experience of being banned from casinos and some whole states because of our dice-control skills that if you throw too much money out there, casinos are going to look closely at you—as they would at any high rollers. Then when your long-term records in their nefarious computers show that you are a consistent and *big* winner over time, well, then you can expect "the tap" on the back and the casino pit boss or shift manager saying to you, "I'm sorry, you are too good shooting the dice at craps. You can't shoot the dice at the craps tables anymore."

Or they might trespass you—a very serious situation. Trespassing goes something like this: "Not only don't we want you to play in this casino today, but the next time you show up you will be considered a trespasser and we will have you arrested." Sometimes they actually read you the trespass law (a truly boring piece of literature) that let's you know what trespassing means and what doing it will cost you.

It is decidedly not a pleasant experience being escorted out of a casino by hulking security guards and snickering casino executives. Yes, they can do that in almost all casino venues. Those casinos are private businesses and—except for cases of racial discrimination, sexual discrimination, and discrimination against the handicapped—you being thrown out on your butt is perfectly within their right.

So if you intend to win a "fortune" at craps using a controlled throw, then here are some words to the wise. Keep your betting at reasonable levels—maybe black chips and no more than purple chips. But don't start within the orange zone, that's asking for scrutiny. You'll win your fortune somewhat slower by betting lower, but you will give yourself the ability to continue to play at your favorite casinos for a longer period of time.

CHAPTER 6

Group and Team Play

Craps is a primitive, communal game. Indeed, the craps table looks something like those ancient altars where animals and sometimes humans were sacrificed. Communities relied on such sacrifices to appease their gods and goddesses and/or to discover what the future held for their tribe and village. Today's craps table sacrifices nothing more serious than players' money but, aside from Darkside followers of the "devil number" (the 7), the craps table sings with combined thrills, hopes, and energy. Usually when a shooter gets on a roll, everyone at the table makes money—yes, their small craps community at that single table has heard the glorious decision of their goddess, Lady Luck, and this decision delights them.

Of course, in the normal run of a craps game, at a table with strangers or some friends, playing a random game, it really doesn't matter who wins or loses money—you basically care about your bankroll. When you shoot the dice in a random game, you and everyone else at the table is rooting and praying and cheering and moaning as Lady Luck plays out her chaotic design because the random game is all about luck and nothing else.

In short, it really doesn't matter what happens because in the aftermath of a good or bad roll, very few craps players feel good or bad for the other bettors after a seven out. That's the nature of the random game. No one has control of anything. Yes, of course, there are ploppies who are royal pains in the asses who think people are deliberately sevening out to screw them. These are people to ignore, if you can.

For controlled shooters, it is a whole different craps game. The group setting can be somewhat dangerous, especially when you first start playing with friends, new and old, at the tables—and most especially if you have told them (or bragged!) about your dice-control skills. The desire to perform in front of them can overcome your concentration and totally screw up your performance. If you bomb in front of these people, will they think you are a crummy controlled shooter? Will they snicker at you or wryly smile that knowing smile that says, "Yes, you are one big bag of bull!"? The pressure is on, and such pressure can be quite distracting for many players.

Both Dom and I have been there. Some players will come to the table, recognize us, and expect us to have devastating rolls every time we get the dice. Unfortunately, it doesn't always happen that way. We've heard laughter and snickers when we have bombed out (yes, all dice controllers bomb out). Some players have actually commented to the effect, "Ha, ha, the Dominator fails. It's all bullshit! You all see that now!" Naturally we don't hear this when we are smoking the tables, but you get the idea. Once you are known as a controlled shooter, a craps game is no longer a regular craps game. It is a whole different animal.

What about several controlled shooters getting together? How about those first few times? Are they tough? Absolutely.

When you start to get involved in a group setting, you and your dice-controlling friends have to make it very clear by saying over and over to each other, "I know you are a good shooter. It doesn't matter what you do. I understand the process and patterns of controlled shooting. Let's have some fun. No sweat." You say it to them; they say it to you. Say it a lot! Over time you will get used to playing craps with each other, and the fear of failure will leave—and your success will become much greater than before because you are now relaxed. Fear of failure tends to predispose us to failure.

Dom and I belong to a team that we call the Five Horsemen (which includes our instructors Stickman, Nick-at-Night, and Skinny), and it did take us some time to become completely relaxed playing with each other; that is human nature. You want to do well in front of your friends, and you shovel on a mountain of self-imposed pressure.

And what about the 5-Count? Using the 5-Count on a friend, particularly if he hasn't yet shot for that session or if his dice aren't looking all that good, is not an insult to him. I've used the 5-Count on Dominator, and he's used it on me. So it must be understood by all your friends (and by you) that it is not a slight if they and you use the 5-Count on each other. We believe that overall, when in doubt, use the 5-Count. Cautious is better than daring in advantage-play craps.

If you have taken the dice three or four times and nothing has happened, you are better off taking a break. Not succeeding on three or four turns in a row has a tendency to mentally wear you out and wind you up. So a short break is in order. If you and your friends have been doing well, going that one extra shooter to see if your streak continues would not be a bad thing. Sometimes long winning sessions can occur. The Five Horsemen once played for over five hours because each of us was hot, and we stayed hot round after round.

Team Play

Team play is the second type of group play and by far the more important and imposing. Here you and your partners are working together, usually with a combined bankroll, in order to snatch that gold tooth from the casino dragon. Most teams are composed of several friends who decide to band their play and their money together and ride each others' coattails. Team play can smooth out some of the variability of the game because you will have several good shooters at the table at the same time.

Setting up this type of team is easy. Everyone contributes the same amount of money into the team's bankroll, and the team plays based on this total. When the shooter has the dice, all he has to worry about is putting down a Pass Line bet with Odds. All other bets will be handled by the other members of the team. The shooter is now free to concentrate on only one thing: shooting those dice.

Obviously, these teammates have to get along, and they have to respect each others' shooting skill—although it is possible that not everyone on the team will shoot the dice during any given session. When combined money is on the layout, some players can get a little tense when joint money is riding on someone else's dice-control skills. This is somewhat strange since your money is riding on others after the 5-Count at times anyway, which is the nature of the game of craps. Still, it seems to be a more powerful awareness when it is a team member shooting. In short, you have to like and have faith in your teammates. You can't be the type who gets easily uptight when your partners or you do poorly. And believe me, there will be times when you and your partners will do poorly.

Now, you can also have a combined team where contributions to the combined bankroll are not the same amount. Here the payouts will be different based on the percentage of the bankroll an individual has contributed. Here too there can be problems. What if the smallest investor has a losing streak of huge proportions? Will his teammates understand the nature of the game and shrug off these losses? Or will they get really upset? These are things you have to consider before creating a team.

There are two other types of teams as well:

- **Financed Teams:** Someone with sufficient funds finances a single player or two or more players and pays a straight salary or a commission based on the team's performance. This can be a dangerous partnership because many of these financiers, while stating they know they can lose, don't actually have that mind-set. Their mouth says they understand they can lose, but their heart is throbbing with anticipation of expected wins, and when they don't win, well, the kaka hits the craps table! Dom and I have been asked hundreds of times to play for the amazingly rich and powerful. Our team, the Five Horsemen, has been asked numerous times as well. Our answer is *always* no. Aside from the fact that we don't need anyone else's money, getting tangled up with other people in these kinds of situations is fraught with peril. We think it is best to avoid this type of team play.

- **Combined *Individual* Team Play:** You and your team members combine bankrolls, but you do not play at the same tables. This type of team can also be a financed one. You play individually at different tables and different casinos and report your wins or losses at the end of sessions or days or weeks. With this type of team, you better have absolute trust in your teammates' honesty. I have seen many blackjack teams become almost armed camps, filled with distrust and hate, when some members have great winning sessions and other members have losing or several losing sessions in succession. Dom and I have played this way many times in craps, and our blackjack teams—composed of very close and honorable friends—have had great success as well. Indeed, our blackjack teams have been going strong for over a decade now. The more individual teams play together, the more wins and losses tend to smooth out as more and more decisions take place; but in the short run good dice controllers can have lousy streaks. If you can handle your teammate falling flat on his or her face, then you can belong to such a team. If you can handle yourself when you fall flat on your face, then you can belong to such a team. If your teammates can handle themselves in those situations, then they can belong to such a team. Still, we think you should proceed with caution when you think of going this route.

CHAPTER 7

Problems with the Throw

Okay, we usually don't want to think too much at the tables, but certain adjustments can be made on the fly without getting too mentally tangled up. Here goes:

Shooting from SL1 or SL2 as a right-hander with a pendulum swing or from SR1 or SR2 as a left-hander with a pendulum swing: Your positioning of the hand is not balanced if both dice go left or right and, just as important, you are sevening out noticeably and often.

If you aren't sevening out much when those dice go astray, go slow with changing anything while at the tables, because the "problem" isn't much of a problem.

Now, at all times in your practice and your play, you want to make sure the dice are square to the bottom of the table, parallel lines if you will. You want to make sure you are throwing the dice down the table in a straight line (or as straight as possible, given your height). The dice will go right or left somewhat because perfect throws are quite rare, but that is not the same thing as both dice scooting all the way one way or all the way the other way.

However, when you read about the *V* Spread in Chapter 10, you should realize that good and excellent throws do not always follow the traditional stopping pattern that dice-control writers harp on. This is important for advanced shooters who might think they are off when, in reality, their throw is right on.

Shooting from SL1 and SL2 as a left-hander or SR1 and SR2 as a right-hander (reverse shooting): As we all know, in the scheme of dice control, this reverse position is usually a far more difficult throw because you really can't use that graceful pendulum swing. Much more muscle power is needed for the reverse throw, and the more muscle power that is used, the more difficult it is to control your throw.

In addition, both dice will tend to scatter somewhat farther right or left even with that parallel positioning of the dice when you are aiming and throwing. When you are practicing at home you *must* shoot the dice from the angle at which you shoot them in the actual casino. So if those dice at a regular craps table must go somewhat less straight to avoid winding up in the corner mixing bowl, then that is how you should shoot in practice at home.

There is no sense in shooting a straight line at home when you can't shoot a straight line in the casino. If you shoot straight at home but at an angle in the casino, you are practicing one thing but needing to do the other thing when real money is on the line. That's like a right-handed hitter suddenly deciding to bat lefty after all his training is the opposite. That angle thing is the most important piece of advice we can give. If you see Dominator's wonderful throw from the reverse position, it is not one where the dice go straight down the table. There is an angle, but that is an angle he practices at home on a regulation craps table. In short, you have to practice at home what you are going to do in the casinos.

Your dice bounce too high on a regular table: We generally recommend shooting at or close to a 45-degree angle. But sometimes those dice tend to go skyward once they hit, which means too much energy is returning into them. If that is occurring, lower the midair angle by small degrees until the dice react favorably by making their slow way to the back wall and dying. On super-bouncy tables, your throw has to be quite low and quite slow to make it to the back wall and bounce back without too much energy destroying your control.

Your dice go in two different directions—one scooting off left, one scooting off right: Generally this is a grip issue. Your dice are not touching each other perfectly in your hand. There is a slight separation, so when they hit they do one of two things. They either bang into each other and that collision sends them away from each other (like two balls banging off each other), or the split makes them hit the table and, without hitting each other, the dice loop opposite ways. When you are gripping the dice, make sure they are together flush against each other and that your thumb is evenly centered on the back between the two dice. The grip can be practiced anywhere—in your office, while you are at lunch, in the bathroom, while stopped at a red light, at dinner with your in-laws, etc. You don't have to be at a formal practice to work on your grip. Without a perfect grip, everything that comes after it will decrease your control, and often the results will be nothing more than random.

But, if your grip is fine and the dice are occasionally landing apart a foot or more *in line with each other* and you still seem to be exerting control, guess what? You are probably in control of those dice just as if they fell backward close together. Just check out the *V* Spread in Chapter 10.

The horrifying double pitch: This is a good sign for on-axis control, which is the necessary ingredient in being able to use radical betting styles in your game. Unfortunately, if you don't correct the double pitch, this is also a bad sign because it means your grip is off just a fraction of an inch, causing one die to spin just a wee bit faster than the other die. Look at the Hardway set, and you see that each double pitch of a die brings up it's opposite. If you have the 5s on top, a double pitch of one die will be a 2. Keep one die on axis but have the other double pitch, and you have that dreaded 7 showing its ugly self. Here the use of a simple mirror on your practice table can help you look at your grip to see if your fingers are straight across the dice. You can also use a handy tool called the Gripper, which will help you get the feel for a correct, straight-across grip.

CHAPTER 8

Handling Degrees
of Surface Bounciness

In our Golden Touch primer dice-control class we use three different types of table surfaces for our instruction: hard, normal, and bouncy. As you go from table to table, you must alter your throw slightly from one type of surface to another type of surface.

However, all of these table surfaces in the primer class fall within what we call *traditional degrees* of bounce—the range of degrees that you will find on most tables in most of the casinos in the country as I write this. On a continuum of traditional craps tables, the surfaces will go from hard to bouncy, but your basic throw and arc angles do not need to change too dramatically, as I will show you. Any problems that occur with your throw can usually be easily corrected.

However, with the new "super-bouncy" table surfaces (synthetic or micro fibor, or traditional fabric padded more heavily underneath)—the handling of which we teach to our advanced classes—some *major* changes have to be made in your throwing style. These have to be made on the run, as super-bouncy tables are unique to themselves and require immediate adjustment. One throw will not fit all of them. On a traditional table surface, we *tinker* with our throw, our energy, our height angle and our spin, but on super-bouncy tables, we *reconstruct* our throws to fit a severely wide range of extreme conditions. With these tables, you have to be alert to the wide range of their bounce characteristics. Some will just be very, very bouncy; some will have "crazy ball" bounces that send the dice flying crazily all over the table; and some others will have dead spots and bouncy spots intermixed.

These super-bouncy tables were not put in to thwart dice controllers but rather to have fabrics that last longer and/or can hold much brighter colors. Interior decorators are more involved in bringing in those new surfaces than executives who know something about what the craps-playing aficionados want.

Can a controlled shooter have success on these super-bouncy surfaces? Yes, absolutely, but doing so requires another set of dice-control skills along with quick, accurate analysis and decision-making. Given a choice between super-bouncy tables and traditional tables, always opt for the traditional ones, because the basic controlled throw is geared to these tables.

Obviously Golden Touch does not teach throws for the super-bouncy surfaces in our primer classes, because that would be totally confusing to someone who hasn't even established any kind of controlled throw yet. You can't run an Olympic sprint if you are still crawling. You have to learn the basics and master those basics before moving up the scale of variability and achievement. So, becoming an advanced shooter does take time and plenty of practice, as many of you reading this know.

However, advanced players should know how to handle these super-bouncy surfaces since we are seeing more and more of them.

Here is a continuum of table bounciness from traditional ranges to the super-bouncy ranges and how to handle them.

Traditional Hard Surfaces: Use your regular GTC throw with several spins and a 45-degree angle with a slight change in your landing zone. You should land the dice as close to the back wall as you can, maybe a couple of inches away, as the table will not fire back much energy on the dice after they land on the surface. When the dice hit the surface, the landing will dull most of the return energy on the dice—just like a brick hitting a brick as opposed to a rubber ball hitting a rubber ball. Then the dice will usually hit the back wall softly and will completely die. You won't usually find the dice doing outrageous landing patterns because hard tables are dead tables. These tables might require a little more initial energy on the dice in order to get them to actually bounce to the back wall instead of landing in a kill shot where the dice do not go forward at all but die where they hit. They just land and stay right there, something the casinos decidedly don't like. A GTC throw with those slight alterations works magnificently on these tables.

Traditional Normal Range of Surfaces: You'll find these surfaces in most casinos across the country. They go from slightly bouncy to slightly hard. Your basic GTC throw with the 45-degree angle works really well on these surfaces because it was structured for them. As you play the traditional surfaces, small adjustments can be made when you see what your dice are doing, but no radical changes will be necessary if you follow all the steps for a good throw: the stance, the set, the grip, the align-ment of the dice with the surface, proper aiming, proper back swing, proper forward throw, normal spin, and flat-on landing (also known as the "smack!" landing). Any small corrections in your throw can usually be made on the spot. You might want to use the first come-out roll with the All-Sevens set to see how the dice react. But on these tables the tra-ditional throw will serve you just fine.

Traditional Bouncy Surfaces: You take your throw down some in terms of the height angle, and you throw with less energy since the surface will shoot back much more energy than it does on hard or normal surfaces. You don't want this return energy from the surface to shoot the dice too fast to the back wall; so your throw must be toned down. The more energy the dice have hitting the back wall, the tougher it is to have control over them when they rebound off the pyramids. Our normal GTC practice rigs tend to have these traditional bouncy surfaces. Shooting softly is the most difficult thing new students must learn to accomplish. Soft is just about always best at just about all tables I have ever seen!

Super-Bouncy Tables: These are starting to be seen in many casinos across the country. Some dice controllers call the super-bouncy tables "trampoline tables," and this is not off the mark.

Some dice controllers think these super-bouncy tables cannot be beaten. This is not so. They can be beaten if you know what you are doing. You must incorporate a new style into your normal GTC throw. Actually you must incorporate *several* new styles, depending on the actual bounce the table is displaying.

Each bouncy table has individual characteristics, and you must quickly and accurately analyze these for your throw to be successful on them.

solve. The backswing on the crazy-ball surfaces might also cause the dice to go berserk.

The big problem with the "extra" and "very, very" bouncy surfaces usually comes *after* the dice hit the back wall. They rebound out and then hit that surface again. Since there is no organized backspin after the rebound to stop the surface from interfering with the trajectory of the dice, those dice are now a victim of the surface, which makes them react harshly by scattering or bouncing or booming them in different directions. To lessen the impact of the rebounding dice after they hit the back wall, those dice have to be thrown much more softly than we throw them on a normal range of tables. And I mean so softly that you would never hit the back wall on a normal surface if you used such a soft throw.

Even if your home practice is on a traditional table surface, to accommodate the super-bouncy tables, you must use a throw that *does not hit the back wall* on these traditional tables. Learning to do this will allow you to throw softly enough on the super-bouncy tables so that the dice hit the back wall at the proper speed—which is close to no speed at all.

So, we are talking now about a low throw, about six inches above the table's surface, with very little energy imparted into the dice to get them to go forward. We are in a "no speed zone" with the force of the throw. If you normally do the Heisman throw with your arm extended out when you are finished, you are now going to go to a trout fisherman's throw, where your arm is flat to the table surface when you are finished throwing. On these super-bouncy tables, the surface will impart plenty of energy when the dice hit it, so don't be concerned that the dice won't make it to the back wall. They will. We need that back-wall hit to be incredibly soft so that the rebounding dice don't have enough energy to make the surface propel them all over the place.

On trampoline surfaces, again you have to lower your throw to about six inches above the table's surface. On these surfaces, you might want to have the dice hit far away from the back wall and take two or three scoots on the surface before they hit the back wall. Give this a test to see if those dice bounce, bounce, bounce in a straight line to the back wall. With each bounce the dice will lose some of their energy...and more of their energy than our normal GTC throw loses. With a super soft throw and several landings, the dice won't bounce much, and when they hit the back wall they should have lost most of their energy. Yes, they will tend to career back more than you are used to seeing—even if you do this throw perfectly—but you will still have control over those cubes by doing the throw properly.

Now, should you find that the two- or three-bounce throw just doesn't work for you—and it might not—then you must launch those dice so softly that you almost think there is no way in heaven those dice can make it to the back wall. Indeed, you should think in terms of missing the back wall, that's how softly you must throw them. Since even the best dice controllers tend to impart slightly more energy into their dice than they realize, trying to miss the back wall on trampoline tables will get those dice to move just right.

Finally, we come to the wild, wacky, weird world of the crazy-ball surfaces. Here we recommend you take a flame thrower and destroy the damn table and then hunt down the deranged individual who created this anti-craps abomination.

Not being able to do that, as murder is against the law, here is how to handle the crazy-ball surfaces:

With a crazy-ball surface, as with a trampoline surface, the dice will look regular going to the back wall. That is, if you accomplish a very low arc with the dice riding straight over the surface of the table at about six inches with a very small amount of energy imparted to those cubes. But once the dice rebound from the back wall, all hell breaks loose. That's when the nutty surface of the table will wreak havoc on the dice.

Can this reaction be stopped?

No.

Can it be contained so that your throw is still able to give you an edge?

Yes.

The key element, working backward from landing to initial throw, concerns the immediate return from the back wall. When those dice hit the crazy-ball surface on their return from the back wall, even small amounts of residual energy will make the surface spring those dice and wheel them in crazy directions, with the dice taking lopsided bounces all over the place. Many of our readers have heard of the expression "dead cat bounce"—which means no bounce. Well, that cat better be long dead after it hits the back wall on crazy-ball surfaces, or it will be given a tenth life!

The low throw, *with almost no energy*, bouncing a couple of times, should hit the rubber surface just under the pyramids. This surface is flat, although at a slightly elevated angle, and with the softest of hits will allow the dice to die with almost no energy remaining, preventing the crazy-ball surface from having much of an impact.

As we said, we want to lower our trajectory on bouncy tables. Our normal stance is to be square to the tables with our shoulders square. To lower our trajectory we want to drop our lead shoulder—right shoulder for right-handers and left shoulder for left-handers. We can accomplish this in two ways.

If we shift our weight to our right foot, we will naturally drop our right shoulder, shooting from the recommended position stick right. Doing this and keeping the same pendulum swing, our trajectory will be lower. For a left-hander, just shift your weight to your left foot. We can also lower our trajectory by starting the dice further back instead of our normal starting position.

Now to lower the number of revolutions (spins), you would move your thumb higher on the back of the dice. To increase the number of spins, lower your thumb.

The Dominator Throw on Bouncy Tables

We have said that you should lower your trajectory from the standard 45-degree angle and reduce the number of revolutions on the dice on these bouncy tables. But Dominator does it differently. He will lower his trajectory but actually put more revolutions on the dice. This seems to work well for Dom.

So the common thread is to lower the trajectory so the dice take a couple of bounces to the back wall, but try increasing or decreasing the revolutions and see what works best for you. To find the proper way to do the bouncy-table throw, you will have to experiment during your practice sessions.

CHAPTER 9

Practice on
Different Surfaces

Confronting super-bouncy surfaces is not something that is easy. You must practice on the various types of super-bouncy surfaces, just as you practice on the various types of normal surfaces. You have to get the feel of a slow—*extremely* slow—soft throw. You have to get the hang of keeping those dice straight as they move slowly through the air. You have to watch carefully as they bounce once (or maybe twice or maybe three times) along the surface, hit the back wall (preferably on the non-pyramid section at the bottom for crazy-ball surfaces), and die.

Interestingly enough, the greatest dice controller of all time, the late Arm, had an extremely gentle, low-arc throw that would have been perfect for these super-bouncy surfaces. Indeed, her throw seemed to work on any type of surface, although during her day the tables all fell into the traditional ranges. Her dice rarely hit the pyramids, which is a preferred landing for the super-bouncy tables. They hit just below the pyramids.

Without practice, you aren't going to be able to defeat the super-bouncy tables, just as without practice you aren't able to beat the normal traditional range of surfaces. Keep in mind something I said before. With a traditionally normal range of surfaces, you can make small adjustments in your regular throw right at the table during a session, and that should be all the tinkering you need. But on the super-bouncy surfaces, small adjustments in your normal throw will have little or no effect. You must restructure your throw. So you have to work on that restructuring in your practice sessions. You can't just do it on the fly.

To that end, we recommend that you buy three or four different types of super-bouncy fabrics and interchange them during your practice sessions. Be particularly alert during your practice to how those dice are reacting after they hit the back wall—that's usually where the trouble will be. Once you get used to your restructured throws, then those noticeable changes in the super-bouncy tables from casino to casino will just require slight changes in your restructured throw.

You should also keep records on the various surfaces to see how your SRR and SmartCraps results stack up against your statistics on the regular range of surfaces.

We do wish there were really easy ways to help you beat the game of craps, but there are no shortcuts. You have to put in the work to give you the shot at getting the edge over the house.

A General Practice Routine

Practice makes perfect. Actually as best-selling gaming author Bill Burton says, "Perfect practice makes perfect." I wish perfection really existed in the world of craps, but there really is no perfection in dice control. There are just too many variables—the table surfaces are all subtly to radically different; back walls are all different, with some pyramids being brand new and others being old and ratty; some pyramids are large, others are small; some are bouncier than others; etc. The air currents, humidity, and temperature will all contribute their own variability to the game. You might be able to get off the perfect shot (or close to it), but that's where it ends. From the release of those dice to the end call by the stickperson, the dice are being hammered by the forces of randomness.

You will end up with control on most shots, but you will never achieve perfection. Just recall how often the dice look perfect in the air, and when the call is made, it's "Seven! Seven out!" You think to yourself, *Those dice were perfect, how could I possibly seven out?* In point of fact, the dice merely *looked* perfect. If you get a super-slow-motion camera you can actually see that throws that appear perfect are far from it.

You can see the effects of, well, *everything* on them. Our eyes can show us that dice control is real—indeed, we can clearly see that when elite shooters are throwing the dice—but our eyes can also fool us into thinking we are seeing perfection when we aren't.

Despite the reality of controlled dice throws being nowhere near perfect, we certainly do have a strong mental image of what the perfect throw and the perfect landing should look like. This mental image is essential for achieving competence and for getting to those elite levels of skill. Perfection is what we hope to achieve when we throw. We work very hard to get our throws as close to that perfect image as we can. Still, achieving perfection is not in the cards, or should I say dice? In dice control, practice makes you have the edge over the casino. The more you practice, then the better your skill and the greater the chance you will turn the tables on the house.

So how should you practice? Obviously, there are no special ways to practice. Some controlled shooters like to set aside a half hour to an hour and just throw those bones. Newer students of dice control will write down their numbers to see what their SRR is. Some experienced shooters often don't bother to write down what faces show; they are merely interested in seeing that all the elements of their throw are done properly.

Dom goes down to the casino in his basement (boy, does he have the life—an actual casino in his basement!) and practices on his craps table. Dom's practice really reflects a craps game. He uses chips to bet; he puts chips in and near his landing zone so he has to be a target shooter. He tries to double his bankroll in a session, or he quits when he gets tired.

My practice is somewhat different. Since I work every day at home, I usually take mini-breaks every hour or so. During those I go to my craps room, shoot until a seven appears or until 15 minutes are up, and then I go back to work. By shooting intermittently I get the feel of a real craps game, where you usually have to wait between your rolls while others take the dice.

However you wish to structure your practice sessions, the overriding concern is simple—you *must* practice or you cannot develop and sustain a controlled throw. Baseball hitters take batting practice almost every day. That's a good lesson for dice controllers.

A Tweak Here and There

There are many elements to a controlled throw. Each one has to be done to the best of our ability because even a theoretical 100 percent perfect initial throw is doomed to have most of its control taken away from it by the time it finishes its journey and the stickperson calls out the number that just landed.

Practicing dice control does not always mean doing everything at once. Since the grip is the most important ingredient in successful dice control, spending time only practicing your grip is a smart idea. You don't have to be at your practice table to do this. Just carry around some dice and when you have a free moment or two take them out and work on your grip.

You can work on just about everything regarding your throw, including the stance, the small backward arm motion, and the pendulum swing without ever releasing the dice. Just do these things as you would do Tai Chi—do the movements in slow motion. Get every aspect down. You don't have to actually throw the dice if you are in environments that won't allow that.

Making each individual element the best you can possibly make it will go a long way to creating a throw that is advanced or elite. You can practice all kinds of throws for all kinds of bounciness. The Tai Chi method of practice is a great routine. I like to do it all the time.

High Flying, Strong Halting, Flat Lining, and Other Things

Many students have asked us about practice tools to help them master the various elements of their controlled throws. There are actually many things you can do for all aspects of performance.

The pendulum backswing from SL1 and SL2 and SR1 and SR2: Golden Touch does not recommend a lengthy backswing. Too many errors can occur once that backswing goes too far back, such as the arm swinging inside. The dice can be launched on too much of an angle so they won't land flat on the surface of the table. If the dice land on the edges, even in a small way, you will see them take weird and crazy bounces or smack into each other, often catapulting the dice in different directions, and you will probably lose all your control.

So let's take a look at the pendulum backswing. As a general rule, you should line the dice right down the middle of your rib cage. Then you lift the dice up a couple of inches, then aim and bring your arm slowly back. You should go back somewhere between six and 16 inches in a straight line and then allow your arm to gently swing, again in a straight line, forward with the dice leaving your fingers in a natural way. Do not force the dice out; nature will take care of that.

If you worry that your arm is going too far back, put some chips in the area you do not wish to cross. If your backswing knocks over the chips, you are going too far back. For lower-arced throws, you will have to release the dice lower in the forward swing. Again, the dice will leave your hand naturally. Just try to do these swings without much thought. Thinking too much can cause trouble—just ask Shakespeare's Prince Hamlet.

Can you move your body on the backswing and throw? Some elite shooters never move anything but their arms; other elite shooters will do a kind of Tai Chi movement with their bodies—slightly back with the backswing and slightly forward with the throw. This movement is extremely small, but it is there. I tend to do the Tai Chi movement. Whichever throw you use—no movement or slight movement—just be completely comfortable with it.

The reverse swing on SL1 and SL2 and SR1 and SR2: The right-hander now shoots from SR1 or SR2; the left-hander shoots from SL1 or SL2. As we stated previously, this throw uses more muscles to achieve its end. You can't bring your arm too far back without dislocating it, so there is a musculature push motion here. The toughest thing is trying to throw straight down the table with this throw. Most of you will not be able to do this unless you are tall, so for many of you, your dice will hit the wall on a slight angle. If you know that in a casino your dice can't hit exactly flush against the back wall, then when you practice at home make sure you are mimicking the casino conditions and not throwing in a straight line. If you are throwing in a straight line, your practice is ingraining a bad habit for reverse shooting.

An advanced way to actually get the dice to hit the back wall flush is to impart a small amount of spin to them. If you are shooting from SL1 or

SL2, you want the dice to be slightly angled on the throw so they make a slight turn to the right as they hit the surface. This turn should level the dice against the back wall. This is not an easy thing to learn how to do, and it will take many hours of practice to get it right. For SR1 and SR2, you want to position the dice so they make a slight movement to the left after they hit.

Here is a strange thing about creating a small curve ball (or "curve dice") when you throw. Most of you will have to see which way the dice should be angled for your particular throw. Some controlled shooters might have to angle the dice slightly toward them; some might have to angle the dice slightly away from them. So this is something you will have to figure out as well. But in this "curve dicing," we are dealing with very small adjustments—you don't want the dice scooting like crazy because you've put too great an angle on them. This is a small, small, small angle.

How to make sure your dice are landing flat: There are many methods you can use to see if your dice are landing flat on the table. You can put a piece of paper down, and if you see dents, then you know the dice are landing on the edges. This will also work with aluminum foil. Seeing a square (which sometimes happens) will mean the dice are landing flat. Another way to judge flat landings is to use sand in a small low-cut box or small dish. If the dice are flat in the sand, chances are they are landing flat on the table. You do not want the sand to be too deep, just enough to assure you can tell a flat landing from a crooked landing.

When you practice your flat landings, you will be using a 45-degree angle (or thereabouts) for the traditional range of surfaces. On super-bouncy tables, you really don't want a strong flat landing; you want a skimming landing that doesn't allow the table's surface to shoot back the dice's energy in a way that causes the dice to really jump or hop all over the place. You can use any of the above methods to achieve this goal too.

A skim will not show the edges hitting the paper if the throw is done properly. Sometimes it is hard to tell if the skim is working because the paper might tear as the dice move forward. This will also be evident on aluminum foil. Wax paper usually allows the skim to take place without any ripping. Ripped paper is not a bad thing; it just causes confusion as to why the paper ripped. You still need flat landings even if you are going for a radical skim. On sand the skimming works really well because you will see the track marks as the dice move forward.

My cup runneth over: All the elite Golden Touch players call themselves "target shooters," because they can hit the same spot on the table over and over. That consistency is an important ingredient in establishing a strong controlled throw.

To work on target shooting, you can use various methods. Many players like to put a small, medium, or large cup in their landing zone. They will try to consistently get both dice in the cup. You do not want the sides of the cup to be too high, just high enough so you can see that those dice are actually going into it. Some shooters like to fill the bottom of the cup with sand or place tissues or cloth into it. You can also use a chip or a small piece of paper in your landing zone and try to hit it time and time again.

Target shooting is absolutely necessary for shooting next to or over chips that have been placed directly in your landing area. Whatever you do, however you *feel*, *do not* ask players whose chips are in your landing area to move them. That's like hanging a neon sign over your head that says, "I am a dice controller! I need to have my landing area cleared of all chips!"

Many of the GTC elite shooters also like to simulate chips throughout their landing area so that they are actually seeing the free spots to land the dice and practicing in a way that mimics playing in a casino.

HIGH-way to heaven: GTC recommends a 45-degree angle as a norm for throws on a traditional surface. Before we get into how to establish this 45-degree angle in practice, we'd like to explain why such an angle is our recommendation.

Think of being on a lake, the surface of the water being an analogy for the surface of the craps table. You want to throw a stone into the water so that it loses its energy when it hits and goes "glup!" right into the water and right to the bottom. How to do this? If you throw at a 45-degree angle when that stone hits the surface, it goes down into the drink. If you throw the stone in as straight a line as you can, it will skip over the water until it loses its power—and that could be four, five, six skips depending on how straight a line you achieve.

So on those traditional surfaces, those misguided advocates who strongly recommend straight-line throws are making it far more difficult for themselves and their followers to achieve any kind of powerful control. The skipping dice have a greater chance to slam into the wall rather than hit it extra softly. They just haven't lost enough energy on their journey. Is it impossible on a traditional surface to have good throws with less or even much less of an arc than 45 degrees? Yes. But it is a much more difficult thing to master. So why do that?

Now, the analogy of the water is not perfect. When the stone hits the water coming down from a 45-degree angle, the water is shooting very little energy back into the stone. The stone just goes straight down, although slowed by the water. But on the surface of a craps table, there is return energy into the dice, and the dice go up as opposed to down. The rebound energy propels the dice to the back wall. Still, given a similar amount of release energy at the start of a throw, more energy will be absorbed by the table on a 45-degree throw than by a straight-line throw.

Of course, all of this is turned on its head when we deal with super-bouncy tables, where a soft, straight-line throw is the best, as this kind of surface will rebound strong energy using that 45-degree arc. Still, it is best to use the best arc on traditional surfaces and the best arc on super-bouncy surfaces—and those arcs are radically different, as you've seen.

So how do you get these arcs?

One way is to use a "high-jump" type of device. You place a straight bar across two poles. Put those bars in such a way that the throw must go over the center bar at a 45-degree angle. To really make sure that the arc is 45 degrees, put your landing bowl or chip or piece of paper where you usually do. This way you cover two very important areas—the arc and the landing.

What if your particular throw does not lend itself to a perfect 45-degree angle? Then change it slowly down until you have the one that best fits you.

For super-bouncy tables, put the bar about eight inches above the surface and throw the dice *under* the bar.

Backward testing: Let me get absurd for a second. The shooter is passed the dice by the stickman and puts them in his saliva-dripping mouth. The casino allows this. He spits them out. They wobble in the air like drunken seagulls. The dice hit the back wall with such force that the spit on the dice flies all over the table and on some of the other players. His stance at the table stinks. His delivery method stinks. His arc stinks. His body stinks. But, damn, his dice die after they hit the back wall, I mean they die *dead*, and he rolls number after number and, more important, this isn't just tonight; he has been doing this for 30 years! He has won a fortune at the table, even though he hasn't bothered to go to the dentist to take care of his black teeth.

Do we change what he is doing leading up to the incredible endings of his throws or just let him do what he does? Despite the hideousness of his performance, the ending is just too good to screw around with all the grossness that leads up to it.

Getting back down to reality, the same can be said about your throw. The *ending* is what counts. As the dice land after hitting the back wall, what do they look like as they come to a halt? If they look damn good, do not, *do not*, mess around with anything that you are doing leading up to that great result.

However, if your end result is not good, then you must take apart the elements of your throw to see what is causing such a disappointing performance.

We always start our search for imperfections with the grip. Maybe 90 percent of our throwing problems are caused by a poor grip. The best grip for most dice controllers is the three-finger grip where your index, middle, and ring fingers are placed on the dice in a *straight line*. You do not want any finger out of alignment. Remember that the ring finger can be a real creator of the double pitch for many controlled shooters.

The thumb is usually about halfway down on the back of the dice with half of the skin on one die and half of the skin on the other die. It does not matter if your entire thumb touches the dice or if your thumb is at a slant as long as both dice get an equal amount of your skin. My thumb just can't touch the dice flush, they touch on the side. I would have to break my thumb and twist it to touch the dice square. Dom's thumb, on the other hand, touches the dice perfectly.

The dice must be flat to the surface, the sides, and the back wall as you get ready to throw. Okay, now throw those dice. Is the final result what you want? If yes, then you have solved your problem. If no, you have to look at the backswing in addition to the thumb and finger place-ment. As you go step by step through the process of finding your flaw or flaws, the end result is the herald that announces, "You got it! Stop changing anything right now." Or it announces, "You need more analysis to figure out why these dice aren't doing what you want them to do."

Although some great shooters actually have a slight angle to their dice as they aim, this is an individual thing. It might happen that as you become more and more proficient you will note that the starting point of the dice is different from the squared-away recommendation we give to the primer students. But always keep this in mind: it is the end result that dictates everything.

This backward testing is a continuous process. You do it in practice, and you do it at the tables. There are so many elements and subelements to a good controlled throw that some problem can always crop up here or there. Baseball hitters sometimes make slight and unconscious changes in their swings, causing a slump; then they have to go over their tech-nique to see what needs to be adjusted. Dice controllers are no different.

CHAPTER 10

Brand-New Information

This chapter contains some more information never before revealed, except in our GTC advanced classes, and this information will increase your awareness and ability to add to your edge over the casinos.

Can the Pyramids Actually Act Like Flat Walls?
The Double-Point Hit!

Many industry writers and other critics of dice control constantly throw this challenge out: "If the dice have to hit the back wall, there is no way the game can be changed from a random one to a controlled one. The pyramids make every throw a random result. Dice control can't possibly work if you hit the back wall."

Many casino pit people, box people, and dealers also believe this is true but, surprisingly, these are often the very same individuals who seem to sweat out good shooters' rolls. This irony is not lost on me. Indeed many casino industry "thinkers" believe that we try to teach our students to miss the back wall in order to make the game not random. Of course, this is not so. You can hit the back wall and win, as we all know.

Certainly the foam-rubber pyramids were put in to assure that the game of craps is random. Dice bouncing off those pyramids get scattered this way and that. The casinos need a random craps game to win money. Random is good for the casinos and bad for the players. We all know this.

However, the game of craps *can* be beaten. For competent dice controllers, the pyramids are merely an annoyance, not a hindrance to exercising dice control. Yes, hitting the back wall of pyramids is not the same as hitting a flat back wall...except sometimes it is *exactly* that. Those pyramids are sometimes the exact same as a flat wall!

Now follow me on this. Here is something you have never read before, because no critics, no craps players, no casino executives, no industry thinkers, and no students—except for those who belong to Golden Touch—know what you are about to learn. On back walls where the pyramids are of small or medium distances from each other, and/or where larger dice are used, the dice will occasionally hit those pyramids as if those pyramids are actually a flat back wall.

Just picture this in your mind. A single die bounces off the layout and hits two adjourning pyramids on their points. The right side of the die hits one pyramid's point; the left side of the die hits the other pyramid's point. That die comes straight back as if the back wall were now a flat wall because a double-point hit is actually like hitting something that is flat.

By hitting in this way, that die will keep most of the non-randomness of your original throw. Your other die might skew a bit, but it will be coupled with a die that has skewed little or not at all.

In fact, elite dice controllers who can keep their dice close to each other will find that sometimes both their dice hit dual pyramid points and both come back to the layout as if hitting a flat back wall.

Obviously such hits will not happen on every throw, but the few times they do happen will increase the dice controller's edge. Those pyramids, while not our friends, are not our mortal enemies either. If you have developed a controlled throw, you know the game can be beaten—even with those pyramids staring you in the face each and every time you throw the dice.

The points of the pyramids can often act as if they are merely flat back walls. Now you know something no one has ever written about.

The Single-Point Pop

A somewhat rarer back-wall hit also makes the back wall behave as if it is flat. This is the single-point pop, where a die will hit one of the pyramids directly on its point and directly in the center of the die. This die will then rebound as if the wall is totally flat. Sometimes you will notice that the single die doing this hit will pop back with somewhat more force than you expected. That's the "stoopball" effect.

Those of you who grew up in cities have probably played stoopball or know about the game. You throw a rubber ball at the stairs of a stoop to propel the ball as far as you can get it to go. If you can hit that ball right on the razor-edge of the stairs and simultaneously in the center of the ball, you will see that ball take off like a Saturn rocket. That rocket is usually a home run too. Since this rocket launch—although obviously far more diminished in craps—exists when you have a die hit squarely dead center on its face and directly on the pyramid point, you might see it return somewhat farther out and then stop a greater distance from the back wall than the other die. This result might not be a home run.

Still, the back-wall-as-flat-wall hit will usually be a primary one—perhaps one that takes place more often than with normal back-wall hits. If both dice hit points, then you have a perfect flat-wall hit. In such a hit, you should see superior results.

Can you practice to get such single-point pops or double-point hits? That's doubtful. The control (and eyesight!) you would need to be able to land a die in these ways is probably beyond those of even the most elite of the elite of dice controllers.

Nevertheless, it is clearly evident that the ruminations of casino industry thinkers, pit personnel, and some dealers have never taken into account these types of back-wall hits. Why should these individuals truly understand the nature of back-wall hits? Pit personnel and dealers are not watching the dice as they hit the back wall to see exactly how these hits are achieved. They just want the dice to hit the back wall, thus following their rules. Once the dice do their back-wall hit, that is the end of their back-wall analysis because no more analysis is necessary on their part.

Casino-industry thinkers rarely play the game or analyze what actually happens in a craps game concerning the nature of back-wall hits. They have no need to, because it is firmly ingrained in their minds that once those dice hit the back wall they will be randomized. And that type of thinking is good for dice controllers.

The *V* Spread: Can the Dice Spreading Out Still Be a Great Throw?

Read all the material on dice landings, and you will note that all dice-control writers (to this point in time) state unequivocally that the dice should stay as close together as possible when they come to a stop after hitting the back wall in order for any degree of control to exist. That does make sense, and I have said the same thing myself many times in articles and books. However, I have actually done a five-year study concerning the results of throws that do not land together but spread out away from each other a foot to two feet, and I have learned a valuable lesson that I will now share with you.

I found contentions that the dice must stop really close to each other to be only partially true. In fact, the dice can also land a couple of feet (more or less) apart and still be the result of a powerful controlled throw.

Let's take a look at a theoretical throw to show how this works. When the dice hit those pyramids, one die can hit on the right side of a pyramid and the other one can hit on the left side of the same pyramid. These dice are merely a fraction of an inch apart, but because they have hit on one side or the other, they will move in different directions. So, let us say that one die takes five rolls going in the right direction before it stops, while the other die takes five rolls in the left direction before it stops.

You now note that they are in a straight line from each other because they have both done basically the same thing. This fact means that the dice are in the same relationship as the dice that stay close together, each taking the same number of rolls, before stopping. Therefore, the dice are in alignment and this is a controlled result.

The above example deals with a perfect shot where the dice do exactly the same thing, but such perfection rarely happens in the real world of controlled shooting. One die will make slightly different motions or movements than the other die. But either close configurative landings or *V* Spreads give the dice the best chance of hitting preferred numbers and/or avoiding the 7. The fact that the dice are not in perfect harmony after they land does not mean no control exists. All dice control is really degrees of control—from okay to stellar. The *V* Spread is a significantly good throw because the two dice are behaving in a similar fashion.

In fact, the *V* Spread is just as good as the close-configuration landing. During your practice sessions you might want to keep a separate SRR for those *V* landings to see how such landings affect your control. I think you will find that *V* landings as just described are every bit as good as close-configuration landings. Keep in mind that the *V* Spread distance between the two dice should be in a straight line or very close to a straight line. Usually dice doing a *V*-type landing, where one is significantly ahead of the other, means the result is probably random.

An example of a perfect *V* Spread result:

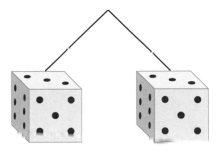

The Sound of *Smack*

Once the dice go up in a 45-degree angle, come down, and hit the table, you can usually hear a sharp *smack!* That sound tells you those dice have hit flush or flat on the layout. That *smack!* is a great indicator that your dice are properly aligned after you throw them, because they are coming down straight and losing a lot of energy into the table.

In the casino, it is sometimes hard to hear that sound because there are so many other sounds at the table that can drown out the *smack!* But in your home practice, listen for that *smack!* If you hear it, you are on the right track when shooting on traditional surfaces. You will rarely hear a *smack!* on super-bouncy surfaces, and that is your first indication that the surface might have to be handled differently from the traditional ones.

Slowly Skipping the Stone

Although this repeats information I gave earlier, it bears repeating. On super-bouncy tables, the 45-degree angle can kill your control because the dice will bounce off the layout with such force that control is virtually impossible. The energy released into the table upon landing will come roaring back into those dice and send them flying, often wildly. On these super-bouncy surfaces, you must skip the dice just as you would skip a stone on top of the water at a lake or ocean.

You will hear no *smack!* or other indication that you are throwing correctly, except your landing after hitting the back wall will be quick and short. However, unlike skipping a stone on water where the faster you throw it the better it is for skipping, the skipping of the stone on a super-bouncy table has to be done slowly...and I mean *slowly*. If you can, try to pretend you are in a slow-motion segment from a movie—yes, actually do everything in slow motion, including releasing the dice.

Slow motion is the only way to play at tables where the dice speed up because of the bounciness of the layouts. It sounds silly, but silliness here will result in a winning throw. You have to allow your dice to be about six inches above the table, floating in the air slowly, so when they take their first bounce they skim the surface, preventing the surface from launching them up toward the back wall.

Learning to defeat the super-bouncy tables will take practice because it is very hard for some controlled shooters to sufficiently slow down their dice's forward momentum. There seems to be a great fear of missing the back wall on these tables by lessening one's energy. Our bodies have been conditioned to throw on traditional surfaces, so now we must also condition them to throw on super-bouncy tables. We have to actually create a new set of muscle memories to handle these new super-bouncy surfaces. It can be done, and many controlled shooters are beating these tables just as they are beating the traditional surfaces.

It takes practice, discipline, and time, but beating those tables can be done, and you can do it.

Dice Correspondence

Super-slow-motion videos of controlled dice rolls will often show a remarkable thing: both dice behaving in a far more energetic way than previously thought when such super-slow motion didn't exist. Such dice behavior includes multiple rolls by both dice. Yet, by studying these slow-motion rolls an interesting fact emerges, and it is this: the dice can be in the same relationships on multiple rolls or pitches as they can be on single and double pitches.

Let us take a look at the Hardway set. If you have the two 3-pips on top and one die pitches twice when the roll is completed and the other die does not pitch at all, you wind up with a 7. That's what is known as "the dreaded double pitch." Now what if one die has four pitches, but the other die has six pitches? You get that 7 again.

Is there a difference in the nature of the roll? Yes and no. Obviously we are dealing with more pitches on the part of the dice, but simultaneously we wind up with the same results. Results are what count.

Dice control can work even with such multiple movements of the two dice as long as those movements correspond to the fewer movements of our standard analysis. This is called "correspondence." A four-roll pitch against a six-roll pitch can still be called a double pitch. You can have far more pitches than just a few.

We have discovered through studying such rolls that many good dice controllers are masters of correspondence. Their dice move a lot, but they are still corresponding with each other. That is the essence of dice control.

Correspondence works in other ways as well. One of the reasons that the Hardway set is the best seven-avoidance set has to do with the correspondence of various results. Five pitches can be the same as a single pitch and so on. As long as the resulting relationship between the two dice remains the same, the number of flips or pitches or rolls is irrelevant because the end results correspond. Again, a single pitch is the same as five pitches. If your pitches are consistent, then you are influencing the dice.

Correspondence has never been written about before, but now you know how and why it works. At first you would think that such multiple rolls would end the idea of dice control. They don't.

But there is even more going on in the world of correspondence.

Double, Double, Toil and Trouble

In all important dice-control literature concerning the Hardway set, we constantly talk about two things that can cause us heartache. The first is the double pitch, when one die pitches twice to bring us a 7 (or actually pitches many times, ending in a result that is the same as a double pitch). You have 3:3 on top with the hardway numbers all around the other faces. Then one side lands on the 3-pip and the other pitches twice, landing on the 4-pip, and up comes a 7.

The second is the dice going off axis bringing us a 7 via 6:1 or 1:6. If only one die goes off axis on a flip or pitch, while the other die stays on axis, then no 7 can show.

Now for the shocking news. There is a correspondence off-axis result that merely looks like an on-axis double-pitch 7. This is called the double flip, meaning that one die flips twice to the side in relation to the other die, while the other die stays on axis or itself flips in a way that it too only looks as if it is on the same axis as where it started. These types of flips on the Hardway set can clearly be seen in super-slow-motion video. Such flips will bring the 7, but the shooter will think he is actually staying on axis and getting the double pitch. Staying on axis is always considered the best thing because, as a shooter's skill increases, his ability to roll certain specific numbers also increases, and if he is a really sharp on-axis shooter he might also be able to bet those Hop bets.

But can the dice be "on axis" when they aren't actually on axis? Technically, no, but essentially...yes. What if a shooter rolls a 4-pip left die all the time, even though this die is flipping? Is he on axis with that die? No. Are his consistent results the same as an on-axis throw? Yes. How do you treat this in terms of betting? You treat it as if it is on axis. Both dice can flip with the results being the same as on-axis results. If the SRR and/or SmartCraps shows these rolls are controlled, then these are (let's have some fun here) off-axis on-axis results.

Let's take a look at the dice in the 3:3 Hardway set and see how these double flips (we use the term "double flip" to include many flips that end up with the same face as a double flip) can mimic double pitches, when in fact they are off-axis results:

Hardway Set: 3:3

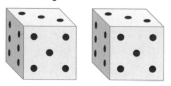

Single Flip to the Right

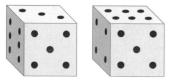

Double Flip to the Right

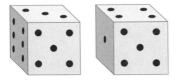

These double flips are the same for all formulations of the Hardway set. Just take two dice, and you will see that this is true.

As more flips occur with both dice, with these results also including some pitches, the tendency is for the dice to become totally random.

Now, if the left die flips four times and the right die flips twice, you get the same 3:4 seven out. Not all shooters using the Hardway set who avoid the 1-pip and 6-pip are keeping the dice on axis. If you have a video camera, record your throw's results to see just how many flips your dice do. This is a great way to tell if you have any control of the dice.

Can double flips not end in disaster? Yes. Just double flip the left and right die, and you come back to the Hardway set. Single flips and triple flips will not bring up the 7 either.

If you are a *consistent* flipper, can you still be a controlled shooter? Yes, of course. If your dice tend to flip once on one side and twice on the other side, no 7 appears. Should you find that your flipping tends to be consistent and does not result in 7s or results in an SRR that clearly shows you have controlled the dice, then these flips are not really harmful, because they show consistency of result. However, if the flips show a random pattern, then these flips mean you are still in the random-roller category.

The Problem with the Language of Craps

You will read or hear these types of expressions all the time:

- "The table is hot."
- "The table is cold."
- "He is having a hot hand."
- "Everyone is sevening out in a couple of rolls."
- "The number 12 [or pick a number or type of bet] is hitting a lot."
- "The number 2 [pick a number or type of bet] isn't hitting."

- "How is the table?"
- "The trend of this table is [choose whatever trend you want]."
- "This shooter is great."

Many craps players base their gambling philosophies on these sentence structures as if the structure is telling us something real about the table at this very moment in time. The belief in these sentence structures is fool's gold, because there is no "is" in the game of craps. There is only "was."

Saying a table *is* hot or *is* cold, or that this or that number *is* hitting or *is* not hitting creates the illusion that these events are in a constant or steady state of existence at the present moment. In fact, none of the above sentences exist in the real world of a craps game.

If you base your betting styles on such illusory sentences you will bet money on future events based on past events. In a random game, these past events do not herald or predict what will happen on the next roll and they cannot predict what will happen "right now." They are completely meaningless.

There is no "is" in the random game of craps. Even controlled shooters will fall into these language traps when they play with random rollers. They will actually believe that a random shooter who *was* hot in the last 10 minutes or half hour or hour will maintain such hotness right now on this throw—that he *is* hot. That is not the case; that is merely the sentence structure of craps talk confusing the real nature of the real game.

What about controlled shooters? It *is* somewhat different for them. Since they are controlling the dice to some degree, which means either decreasing the appearance of the 7 or increasing the appearance of certain specific numbers, one can make a future statement based on the skill of the shooter, such as, "This shooter has the skill to continue to hit a number of 6s over the random probability." Thus, you could, if you wish, make a statement such as, "He is skillful," because that skill does exist at this moment in time and the next moment as well.

It all comes down to using the proper verb tense in the game of craps. That will focus your mind on the truth of the game, not the illusion of the game. There is no present tense in the random game. If you understand that the sentence structures of the random game are misleading, you will not fall into the typical betting traps most craps players plunge into. Those of you who are truly skilled and serious players must knock the false "time code" out of your minds. *Is* is dead!

The language of craps is misleading—it *is* misleading right now, and I am guessing it will continue to be misleading into the future, to the detriment of the players.

CHAPTER 11

End Throws, No-Dice-Set Casinos, and Throw-Them-Harder Ploppies

End Throws

Golden Touch has always taught a simple concept about dice control: it is best to shoot from the closest points to the back wall. Such points are SL1 (stick left one), SL2 (stick left two), SR1 (stick right one), and SR2 (stick right two). We use as our analogy that it is easier for a pitcher to throw from the pitcher's mound than from second base. His control will be far better doing so, as will his consistency.

This is not a false statement, but it is not entirely the whole case.

There are end shots that can gain the dice controller an edge over the casino. These end shots are nowhere near as good as the above "close-point" shots for obvious reasons. More power must go into the end shots, and those shots are far more muscle-related pushes than swing-related releases as with the SL1, SL2, SR1, and SR2 throws. Muscle throws are much harder to control than pendulum-swing throws.

End shots also require far more energy to be put on the dice to get them to the back wall, and such energy results in a greater bounce back when the dice hit the pyramids. If the dice come off the back wall faster they will hit the layout further back and bounce with more force. The more energy on the dice the more things can go astray in controlled shooting.

In Golden Touch we do have many good end-shot shooters, but their SRR and SmartCraps results from the end of the table are not quite as good as their close-point shots. This is even true of the great Dominator, who has one of the best end-shots I have ever seen. Of course, lesser performance from end shots does make sense. No one would claim—*no one sane*—that an end shot is better than a close-point shot.

So how does one accomplish a decent end shot? Practice the following steps:

1. Stand square against the table.
2. Stand on your tip toes.
3. Set the dice, usually in the Hardway set unless SmartCraps gives you a specific set to use.
4. Put your non-throwing hand on the chip rail to help you get up as high as you can.
5. Your throw could have a little backswing if that makes you feel more comfortable. That means you put your hand out a little more so you actually can take it back as a part of your throw.
6. Go forward so that by the time your throw is complete your arm is in a straight line.
7. Release your dice just as your arm gets to that straight-out position.
8. You might have to put slightly more spin on the dice to retard their hitting the back wall too hard and bouncing off the pyramids.

If this throw is performed properly on 12-foot tables, your extended arm will be about at the SL or SR 2.5 or 3 position. You must make an effort to reduce the power behind the throw, which is not as easy as it sounds. As you aim down the table, you have to think of everything in a straight line. Your arm goes out in a straight line, the dice fly through the air on a straight line, and they hit the flat part of the back wall.

As with all controlled throws, it will take practice and recording your results to make sure you actually do have an edge from an end-shot position.

Using a decent end-shot player when you take over a table is a good idea. If you have 12 of your own players at a table, just having the four close-point shooters throwing the dice could look a little suspicious. Using two to four end-shot shooters makes your group far more like a normal group of friends having fun playing together.

No-Dice-Set Casinos:

Some casinos here and there across the country have banned shooters from setting the dice. They want the shooters to just pick them up and throw them. Their reasoning is probably twofold:

- Too many dice setters, be they random rollers or controlled shooters, take too long to set and therefore slow down the game.
- Some casinos are terrified of shooters who do have the skill to control the dice.

The executives of these casinos have mistaken notions that without dice setting all aspects of controlled throws are thrown off. Just as the notion that controlled shooters are deliberately trying to miss the back wall or that the pyramids of the back wall automatically make the results random, the notion that preventing shooters from setting the dice destroys dice control is false.

A shooter with good on-axis results, somewhere in the 48 percent or above category, can gauge his betting based on what numbers the dice are set in when the stick person passes them. Obviously, you must have a Pass Line or Don't Pass bet up to shoot, but you don't have to make any other bets until you get the dice. The shooter is usually given a respite from the rule that you can't throw in late bets after the dice are out. You will then base your betting on the faces you see (you can do the faces you don't see that are on the axis, but you might have to think too much to do that).

For example, here's what to do if the dice have a 5-pip and a 1-pip on top, with a 4-pip and 4-pip facing you, like this:

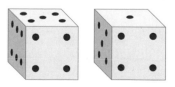

You throw out your bets on the 6 and the 8. If your on-axis throws are good enough based on your mathematical or SmartCraps analysis, you can make Hop bets on them too.

By jumping on the set that the dealer gives you, the casino's rules are being followed, but you are simultaneously basing your throw on a dice set. Is this the best way to play? Of course not. But given no choice and also given no other venue in which to play, then use the "dealer set" as your set and bet accordingly.

Paranoid Ploppy Says, "Throw the Dice Harder!"

Yes, there are some ploppy box persons, floor persons, and pit bosses who jump on some dice setters for not hitting the wall hard enough. I have not seen any ruling by any casino-control commission in any state that says how hard the dice have to hit the back wall. Still, these folks run the game. There is no getting around the annoyance of such paranoid ploppies.

There is only one solution for such casinos. Leave them. It isn't worth an argument over the idea of what is or isn't a hard enough throw or a big enough bounce off the back wall. Random rollers might be throwing far softer than you, but they don't come in for any heat from the casino. Is it fair? No. Is it the casino's right to do so? Yes. Again, leave and take your business elsewhere.

CHAPTER 12

The Patterns of Dice-Control Performance

Which of these statements is true?
1. "I take the dice, and every time I get them I win some money on my throw.
2. "I take the dice, and I go on a roller-coaster ride."

Unless you are a divine being from Mt. Olympus, no one—and I mean no one, including the staggeringly great lady who was known as the Arm—wins every time he or she gets the dice. The uniquely gifted Arm had the best throw I ever witnessed, but even she had losing hands with the dice. (Full disclosure time: I actually don't remember many of her hands being losers.)

Working our way down from the Arm, if you are a competent, good, advanced, or elite dice controller, then you know this: you are in an up-and-down game at the craps tables. That's the nature of the beast— volatility—like a roller coaster. You will not win every time you get the dice. You will have streaks of losing, too, and some of these streaks will feel like they will never end. That certainly can be depressing, and dice depression is not good for a dice controller's focus on the game.

A random roller is also in an up-and-down game. He'll have some winning sessions and he'll have some losing sessions, but sadly over time his losses will mount up and his bankroll will dismount. For a random roller it is up and down and up and down and up and down and down and up and down and down and down and up and down and down—and the casino wins the prize, which is the random roller's money. His line of activity goes slowly down the drain.

For a controlled shooter, just follow the pattern of the random roller in the above paragraph, but change all the *ups* to *downs* and all the *downs* to *ups*. At the end of a decent period of time, a controlled shooter will have taken the money from the casinos. The edge has now shifted to the player. His graph is going up over time.

However, since the patterns of a controlled shooter's won/lost performances are so volatile, many casino bosses—seeing the best controlled shooters (such as my team, the Five Horsemen) having miserable sessions—smugly figure that such a thing as an advantage-craps player does not exist. That's good. We prefer not convincing anybody that dice control exists. I know it does from experience. You know it does from experience. I know it does from SmartCraps results, and you may know this as well.

Luckily, to help this illusion that dice control doesn't work, at the tables there are many dice setters—those who have no actual dice-control skills—throwing the dice. Also, there are many adherents to weird dice grips who have no (or little) influence over the dice and also those wild-eyed, feverish adherents of rickety dice theorists who will recommend all manner of nutty losing betting methods in order to get the edge over the house. With so many bad controlled shooters—now known as "uncontrolled shooters"—plying the felt (or other fabrics) and with all the betting systems out there, a natural camouflage has been developed.

Now if you check our website at http://www.goldentouchcraps.com/worldrecords.php4 you will see an impressive number of GTC members who have had rolls of 40 or more numbers before sevening out. Note how many have gone over 50 and 60 rolls before sevening out—truly remarkable achievements all witnessed by others, as well. Indeed, we have many instructors and students who have gone over 70 and 80 rolls of the dice before sevening out. Such monster rolls, while laudatory, are not the sole or sufficient reason for our long-run winning play. Indeed, the consistency of rolls in the teens comprises the foundation for a controlled shooter's long-run victory over the casinos. That and rolls where a number is repeated in succession before a quick seven out. Throw in a share of rolls in the 20s and 30s, and you have a winning controlled shooter.

There are some interesting speculations about how controlled shooters differ from random rollers in other ways. Most of our novice and intermediate shooters use the Hardway set, a seven-avoidance set, and when their shot is off the belief is that the number they are setting to protect against will be the number that comes up more. You set against the 7, your throw is off for whatever reason, and the 7 comes up more than the normal 16.67 percent of the time in such cases. So, using a baseball analogy, controlled shooters tend to be home-run hitters, and home-run hitters tend to have more strikeouts than singles hitters. If you happen to be at a table with many controlled shooters, you will see strikeouts, but you will also see many repeating or some strong or even monster rolls.

While the use of the Hardway set is excellent for shooters with little or no on-axis control, dice that double pitch or flip twice in relation to each other can cause all sorts of problems. But the Hardway set will protect against all single deviations in dice landings. As a shooter gets more on-axis control, SmartCraps will probably recommend other dice sets for your personal use as shown in the radical betting sections of this book.

Controlled shooters also have a self-destructive pattern as well. If you are a random roller, you shoot the dice, say a prayer, and hope you don't seven out. (Or as a Darkside "don't" player, you hope you do hit the 7 and not the numbers.) If you are having a rotten day, you chalk it up to bad luck, and while you are not happy about losing money, you figure that is the way the game is. The casino wins, the player losses, and all is right with the world. For random rollers, losing is expected and winning is ecstatic.

For many controlled shooters (perhaps most controlled shooters), winning is expected and losing is always devastating. So when a controlled shooter wins, it is not as big a thrill to him as losing is a downer. The intensity of emotion when you lose is far greater than the intensity of the joy when you win. The random roller, who expects to lose, is in heaven when he wins because winning is really not what he expects. The controlled shooter feels right when he wins but absolutely miserable when he loses.

I joke in our dice-control classes that once you start learning how to control the dice, craps loses a lot of its joy, even though you are now winning money. It becomes more work than leisure. Your skill *and* your ego are on the line each and every time you get those dice. The random roller feels no such thing. He's the dupe of fate, where the controlled shooter has taken fate into his own hands.

Dealing with Slumps

The worst thing that can happen to a dice controller is hitting a big slump. It doesn't matter if you are an elite or advanced controller or just an adequate one, slumps are inevitable. I've been there, Dom's been there, every member of the Five Horsemen has been there. In fact, the Five Horsemen have had some occasions where all five of us hit the wall the way marathon runners do—and we hit it at the same time. These sessions weren't pretty, and they didn't feel pretty either. It was so bad one time—and I was so bad when I shot the dice—that I wanted to go back to my room, curl up into a fetal position, and suck my thumb.

Dom and I have never gotten used to slumps. We can't stand the big ones; we can't stand the small ones; in fact, we can't even stand a single losing turn with the dice. Sadly, too many controlled shooters allow slumps to get inside their heads and throw them off. They've had a bad day, the next day is also a bad day, and so is the next one after that. Now the horrible thoughts creep in: *Have I lost my touch? Am I now just a random roller? Will my results continue to stink from this point on?* Do such thoughts help the controlled shooter perform better the next time out? No, they just add stress to the next day's playing sessions.

If you use the meditation and visualization techniques outlined in Chapter 14, these should help relax you when you come to the tables. In point of fact, you aren't in need of your craps money to make a living. Almost all controlled shooters are "avocationalists"—this isn't their job, and they don't need the money for their heart operations or little Timmy's college education. So, since the money—while important—isn't really needed, just say to yourself, "To hell with the past. Each day is another day. I am playing a game; the game shouldn't be playing me. Now I'll go to the tables and have some fun!"

Yes, I know I said that craps has been ruined because we are now concerned with a skilled activity; but the more you can convince yourself that this skilled activity is also a fun activity, the better chance you will have to shrug off slumps and *end* them. I don't think any controlled shooter is ever free of feeling bad because of poor performance, but it is necessary to prop yourself up when these performances occur. Just say to yourself what you would say to a dice-controlling friend and then listen to yourself and take your own advice.

My wife, the beautiful AP, jokingly says, "Take my advice; I'm not using it." Well, give yourself the right advice, and then use it.

CHAPTER 13

Betting, Emotions, and Friends

When I write articles and books for average gamblers or novice and intermediate advantage players, I am extremely careful to give clear, concise, and—I hope—wise counsel on money management, betting styles, and the house edge in terms of percentages and money. Caution is the key to all my advice. But a book about advanced strategies, many of which have been held in secret by the elite dice controllers, takes me in a different direction entirely.

Obviously, you have read sections of this book showing that traditionally horrendous bets can actually be better than traditionally good bets for dice controllers with superior on-axis ability. I leave it up to you to decide whether to incorporate such radical betting styles into your play. If you are good enough, then go for it if you wish. It is your decision. You will, in a sense, be leaping off the high diving board. Others have made the transition to radical betting—or at least to partial radical betting. Even I, known as Mr. Cautious to my friends, have done radical betting—but never when there are students or anyone who knows me at the table. That would give a very bad example if they didn't know what was really happening in my particular game.

Dominator is completely different. He doesn't care who is at the table or whether they get the wrong idea about what he is doing. His attitude is that they can ask him what is going on if they are interested. Of course, almost no one asks him. He has an intimidating persona. So, as

I stated previously, they ask me. I tell them the untruth about why Dom bets as he does because I don't want them getting the ridiculous idea that they can or should bet as Dom does on himself and on other elite shooters. It is a helpful little "white" lie that I formulate to prevent the unwary, unsavvy players from causing their bankrolls to go into the red because they wanted to mimic an elite player.

Still, being one to always offer advice, I can't help myself in cautioning anyone interested in taking the plunge into radical betting styles to make sure that he does have the kind of on-axis control necessary to go after these otherwise awful bets. If you are good enough, you will make quite a lot more money over time than you would by simply betting the traditionally best craps bets.

Going Between Radical and Traditional Betting Styles

Truth time: I just can't do a steady diet of strictly Hop bets with no other bets on the layout other than my Pass Line with full Odds so that I am allowed to shoot. Yes, I'm scared to use only Hop bets. This is an *unreasonable* fear, but it is real. I've sometimes referred to myself as a "chicken gambler," and that is what I am. I find it hard to overthrow my thinking to go for those Hop bets exclusively. Some advantage players might scoff at me giving in to fear, but if I didn't acknowledge that fear and instead forced myself to play through it (if that were even possible), I know my throw would quickly deteriorate because of my nerves.

I would be thinking too much, and thinking is bad when you are trying to allow your body to do what you have trained it to do. Thinking too much interferes with your muscle memory, causing an intellectual spasm to exist. That spasm takes away from your throw. That intellectual spasm is as real as a muscle spasm. Just try shooting the dice as you pump your arm muscles up. You'd be lucky to get the dice to even look as if they came from a good dice controller.

My on-axis throws are statistically at the top level of performance, based on SmartCraps and pen-and-paper analysis. When I took the three SmartCraps tests the very first time and passed all three (not an easy thing to do), I was told that the correct set for me, based on my on-axis percentage using the Hardway set, was the 3V. Of course, for over two decades the 3V is the set I have used almost exclusively, with occasional fallbacks into the Hardway set if my dice were not behaving properly. I hammer the 6 and 8—with the 6 being the stronger of the two since my hard-6 hits occur way out of proportion to random results. Perhaps that's because I have the 3V set up with the two three-pips on the top, and quite often my dice stay on axis just as I set them in my grip.

Even with a strong on-axis performance I just can't go exclusively with the radical Hop betting. So I mix it up. I will place the 6 and 8 whenever I throw—or I will just place the 6—and then I will Hop the hard 6 for far less money than what I put on a Place bet. I am *comfortable* betting this way. Is this the correct mathematical way to bet with my on-axis results? No. But it is the correct way for me. I am not a gambling writer who dismisses the very real role that emotions play in our advantage over the casinos.

If you are at the table with Dominator and he is going after those radical bets, he too will spread his bets on the numbers, either Placing and/or using the Come with Odds. Both of us have edges on those Place bets, so why not make them as we have done for over two decades? Such traditional play also goes with a lifetime of training and allows us to think of our radical bets as just additions to what we already do.

Now, it is possible that with the passing years I will lose my hesitancy and just go whole-hog for the Hop bets, but I do not see that scenario in the near future. So if you are hesitant to attempt the radical betting styles in an exclusive way—then don't do it. Your emotions count as a controlled shooter. That's a fact.

The Problem with Emotions

As stated, human beings are emotional creatures. We can't escape it. At craps you will see emotion clearly displayed when players cheer, shout, and high-five or moan, groan, curse, and storm away from the table. Craps is about as primitive a table game as you can get in the casino, and with primitiveness comes high-intensity emotions. Such emotions are contributing factors to players losing sight of how to play properly.

Most gambling writers will state unequivocally that craps is the most exciting game in the casino. I share that opinion. However, I do not think it is exciting because you make bets, win bets, or lose bets. Making, winning, and losing bets occur at all casino games.

When I was an actor, I was well aware that the more people in the audience the better the chance I would get laughs while performing a comedy. People in large groups tend to let loose more than they would in small groups. They lose inhibitions, and thus they laugh out loud more when other audience members are laughing with them.

This "group rule" holds true for craps. When 10 to 14 players are at a craps table and things are going right, there exists a communal energy that flows from one person to the next to the next. Rational thought becomes subsumed within an emotional response to what's happening in the here and now. In short, people develop a group consciousness. They cheer and laugh and applaud and shout as a hot shooter makes number after number. They moan in unison when that same shooter finally sevens out. They are as one.

Because of the communal energy at the craps table, many random players lose sight of what bets to make and what bets to avoid. Since most craps players tend to make a wide range of bets, most of these bets having high house edges, relatively astute and conservative bettors are sometimes drawn into also making such bets because the group or communal consciousness has taken them over. It's the gambling equivalent of *Invasion of the Body Snatchers*.

So it is not inconceivable to think that the communal consciousness at a craps table is a contributing factor to casinos making more money at the game than they would if each player were merely playing one-on-one against the house. I'm guessing that fewer bad bets would be made by random players, more good bets would be made by them with one-on-one play against the casinos, and the game would move along like blackjack or other table games where you rarely hear people cheering and clapping. Those games are individual games, not communal ones.

Now, I enjoy the camaraderie at the craps table just as much as other craps players, but I have locked my emotions against trying to make a killing by wagering on bets I can't beat on shooters who have no dice-control ability—which are almost all shooters at the game. I will cheer, applaud, and shout with glee when numbers are being hit, but I don't care if those numbers are on bets I am avoiding such as the Horn or Whirl. Its fun for me to clap and cheer, but it is not fun for me to lose money.

While I can get emotionally carried away like any craps player, I will not let my money get carried away.

One lesson I have learned is to treat outcomes that I am not wagering on as if they don't exist. If I am not betting on the 11 and the 11 is hit by the random shooter, I do not think, *Gee, I wasn't on the 11. I could have won money if I were.* Instead, I think that nothing happened. That roll was merely dead time. If the 11 is hit again, it is just more dead time. I only think about the decisions that concern me—the Pass Line and Come bets with Odds, or my Place bets of the 6 and 8, or my own Hop bets if I am shooting. Nothing else matters to me.

I know this is a hard lesson to learn. It actually took me several years to learn it. But numbers at craps games all over the country are hitting right now, but I'm not on them. I'm home writing this book. Now, if I were at those tables and numbers hit that I wasn't on, so what? They mean just as much to me as the number that hit somewhere in the country just as I type this period at the end of this sentence.

The Captain of craps, the legendary Atlantic City player and my gambling mentor, once told me, "The contest isn't between you and the casino; it is between you and yourself." At craps tables that have been "hot," the "yourself" might just overcome "you" and cause you to lose sight of what is the right way to wager your money. As an advantage-craps player, you must wager based on your knowledge of your SRR and/or SmartCraps results. To do other than that is to court disaster.

Allowing the joyful experience of a communal consciousness and response to a craps game to totally wipe out your better judgment is probably the most dangerous aspect of the game for random rollers and for advantage players. Once you are carried away, once you allow yourself to throw caution to the wind, you are asking for trouble.

So, yes, enjoy the game of craps, enjoy the camaraderie of the other players, but make sure you keep control of your betting and your bankroll. Don't get carried away by the fact that others have been carried away.

Remember what your mother probably said to you: "Just because so-and-so is doing thus-and-such, is that why you are going to do that? Do you always have to follow the crowd?" That's a good lesson to learn.

The Emotional Impact of Playing with Friends

To paraphrase—and totally ruin—a great quote: "It is a wonderful thing to lose your bankroll for a friend." And this is often what happens when you play with friends who are random rollers and, even more important, when you play with friends who are also controlled shooters.

Friendship is a wonderful thing, nobody will deny that, but sometimes such wonderfulness causes advantage-craps players to lose sight of why they are playing the game. The reason you go to the table is not to be with your friends. You can be with them at meals, at the swimming pool, driving to the casinos, going to movies or plays, meeting each other over at each other's houses. Companionship is fine at the craps tables too. You have someone to shoot the breeze with when you are not shooting the dice or when they, if they are controlled shooters, are not shooting.

But in no way, shape, or form are you to play to impress your friends or, worse, try to win them money. How many advantage-craps players, especially new ones, have had this conversation with a friend or relative? You may have had it as well.

You: I just took a course in how to control the dice. I can now beat the game of craps.

Friend: No one can beat the game of craps.

You: I can. It can be done by using the proper throw and betting properly.

Friend: Baloney. No one can beat the game of craps.

You: I can.

Friend: Okay, let's go to the casino, and you show me.

You: That fine.

Friend: Fine.

You: You'll see.

Friend: I can't wait. We'll become millionaires after our next visit if you can control the dice, which you can't.

You: You'll see that I can.

Now our advantage player is in the casino at the table getting the dice passed to him by the stick person, and he *must* perform. He is totally aware that he *must* perform—not just for himself but for the friend(s) he bragged to about his newfound controlled-shooting skill. The advantage player is close to being a nervous wreck. If he has a good roll it probably has little to do with skill and everything to do with luck.

It can be even worse when several controlled shooters go to the tables, especially for the first or second time. Each one wants to show off to the other ones. These are the worst emotional situations a controlled shooter can get into. The thought that everyone is looking at your throw, analyzing it, critiquing it in their heads, is enough to strip the advantage player of any advantage he might have.

As stated, I certainly never dismiss the impact of emotions on a controlled shooter. Those emotions are real and powerful, and they affect everything you do. If you have friends who are random rollers, don't brag to them about your skill. Just tell them you are going to practice what you learned, but you know you can fail at it, just as any craps player can fail. Or don't tell them anything at all. Why do they have to know you are a controlled shooter? Silence might just be golden here.

Should your random-rolling friends note that your throw looks different, just shrug and tell them you are trying to shoot in a way that looks good. Now, should they begin to win money on trips with you then, yes, you can reveal that you are indeed a controlled shooter and maybe even recommend that they learn to do it themselves. Don't be disappointed if most won't take the time to learn how to beat the casinos. It's just too much work for casino gamblers who usually rely on luck in their gambling games.

And don't get sucked into being their opportunity to win money on a regular basis by them hitching their wagons to your star. You might find your random-rolling friends constantly harassing you to go to the casinos with them so they can take advantage of your rolling skills. This can be annoying and harmful to your throws, as you will be shouldering your own and their bankrolls. Silence is often golden when you have the golden touch at craps.

If you have a group of dice controllers as friends and you are going with them to the casinos for the first time, all of you should speak honestly about your nervousness in performing before each other. Such a talk will help remove some, though not all, of that nervousness. They will be as nervous as you are. It doesn't matter if you are a new controlled shooter, an experienced one, or a member of the advanced or elite classes, being with other controlled shooters for the first time can be nerve-wracking.

At the table for the first few rounds, you can also make smaller bets than normal so that the economic impact of a poor performance before the crowd is not too great. Also do not hesitate to use the 5-Count on your random-rolling friends or on your dice-controller friends as well. You'll probably save yourself a fortune since those dice controllers are probably just as nervous as you, and those random rollers will always and ultimately lose you money no matter what you do or how you bet. The 5-Count will be your safety net.

Keeping Your Cool at the Tables

In any casino game that you play with other people at the table, there is always the chance that you'll metaphorically rub shoulders with persons whose shoulders you'd prefer they keep to themselves. Slot players don't usually have to worry about disgusting, ill-mannered, unkempt, unclean, and obnoxious players standing right next to them, slobbering on them, because slot players can move from machine to machine should some shaggy beast sit at the machine next to them. The slot player's life is just him or her and the machine. It's an intimate relationship.

Not so with craps players. Yes, the craps tables attract many decent, nice, and personable players, the majority of whom are a pleasure to play with at the tables. But craps also attracts troglodytes—unevolved creatures whose only goal in life is to annoy and disgust you. These people are also known as ploppies, and they prove the un-Darwinian theory of devolution.

It is not the casinos' fault that some people are mangy monsters. Any place that caters to the public has denizens of the night (or morning or day) attracted to their premises—be these premises restaurants, bars, grills, or libraries. It's the way of humanity. Behind us are creatures it is best not to turn around and look at.

I've seen plenty of gross things at the craps tables. During many of my monster rolls, from 50-handers to my all-time record of 89 rolls, there have been stinky-breath players who have decided to talk into my nostrils—their smelly breath causing acute nausea in me as I try to concentrate on what I'm doing, which is attempting to take the casino's money.

"Hey, hey, ha, ha! Ho! Ho! Go! Go!" one beer-swilling sot shouted into my nose. All those words ending in "a" and "ey" and "o" were killing my olfactory nerves. Is there a law of nature that forces those with hideously bad breath to fire it up other people's nostrils? Shouldn't that be considered a crime against humanity?

I've been slammed on the back so hard during long rolls that had I been Quasimodo I wouldn't be able to call myself the hunchback of Notre Dame anymore. And I certainly did not want to high-five that sallow-faced guy's hand, whose digits displayed some kind of weird red-purple skin eruptions.

I don't particularly care for people blowing cigarette smoke into my face, and I especially can't take cigars—be they Cuban or otherwise—wafting into every pore of my body. But worse than tobacco smoke are those barbarians who chew tobacco! My Lord! Not only are their teeth a horrible brown color, but they spit their mouthfuls of gooey gunk into coffee cups and plastic glasses—right there, right there at the table, next to you. Spit! Slop! Spray!

I like a drink when I am in the casino, maybe even two drinks. But I can't stand drunks, and I really can't stand loud drunks, and I really, really can't stand loud drunks who are not funny but who think they are funny. These loud "comedians" figure if you didn't roar with laughter at their latest witticism it was because you couldn't hear it over the din of the casino. So they shout louder than a jet breaking the sound barrier, as if enhanced decibel levels will make their idiotic comments sound funny. I don't want non-jokes shouted into my eardrums and blown up my nose.

Here is something that truly irritates me—women of age (okay, okay, women over 30) who pretend they are "wittle gurls." Come on! What is with this little-girl act? Who the heck is interested in a 50-year-old eight-year-old?

Finally, I really don't want to be given unsolicited advice at the craps tables by experts who don't know their ankles from their asses. There are some ploppy players whose sole goal in life seems to be to annoy all the other players at the craps table by boisterously proclaiming how everyone should bet. One will say, "You see the 12 has come up twice in a row, so it is now due to come up again. Everyone get their money on the 12!" He'll say to me, "Hey, buddy, why ain't you betting that 12? It just showed a couple of times."

I simply shrug, but what I'd like to say is, "^%*&!!!@()*&^%:;***!!!!!!"

I will leave it to your imagination as to what "^%*&!!!@ ()*&^%:;***!!!!!!" means, but it isn't nice.

I have left out the bodily fluid stories coming from areas where bodily fluids can leak, flow, or squirt out of a person's body. I am sensitive to the refined sensibilities of my readers, so I will not get graphic about these events (even about the one where a drunken loudmouth pissed on the leg of a female dealer in a downtown Vegas casino).

I am sure many of you also have your dislikes at the tables. But craps is still too much fun to play to allow the devolved ploppies to make the game unsavory for us—even if they are themselves unsavory.

I also tend to be calm even in the face of bad breath into my nostrils, tobacco spitting that splats, loud yelling into my ears, and strong power slaps on my back. But if Dominator has a flaw in his game, it has to do with his temper when faced with ploppies who interfere with his game. Yes, he can lose it at times.

One Monday evening in Las Vegas with the Five Horsemen, Dominator had a 39 roll and then fell flat on his next two hands. That was fine, as his 39 had been number after number—a typical great Dominator hand. We made money, nice money, on that roll. I took the dice three times as well. The first two times...well..."sucked" is too kind a word to describe my shooting.

There was a young man in the proverbial baseball cap standing near the dealer on the end of the left side of the table. He wasn't betting; he was just watching. I didn't know him. He wasn't a student of Golden Touch but was just some baseball-capped kid watching the Five Horsemen stink up the craps table. He had not been at the table to see Dom's 39 roll.

After my second disastrous roll, the baseball-capped kid said, "Hey, Frank, based on an analysis of your dice, I would recommend using the V2 set, not the V3 set."

Obviously, while I didn't know him, he knew me. I couldn't believe he just shouted this across the craps table at me. Also, I had shot two point/ seven outs. How the hell could anyone analyze anything on such a short sample? And it is 2V and 3V; not V2 and V3!

The dealers and box person all knew us at this high-end casino, and they would cheer when we hit numbers because 1) We tip a lot and 2) We are nice guys to deal to and deal with. They were also surprised that this baseball-capped cretin shouted his recommendations across the table.

As is my way, I ignored him. Not Dominator. He moved back from the table, looked at the baseball-capped kid, and said, "What the fuck!" I don't think the capped kid heard him. Dom took the dice and quickly sevened out.

Then the dice went around the table—Skinny, Nick-at-Night, Stickman, and me sevening out quickly—and Dominator got the dice. Dom sevened out quickly too. And then it happened.

The baseball-capped kid said, "Dom, let me give you some advice about your shooting." Dom looked at him, his face totally surprised. The kid continued, "I can help you shoot better. I see the flaws in your shot."

Now, Dom will take advice from advanced and elite shooters he respects (such as the members of the Five Horsemen). We all will. But who was this baseball-capped kid to give the great Dominator advice? The box person rolled his eyes and looked at me and shook his head as if to say, "This kid is an idiot!"

Dom—his face puffed red with the veins on his scalp pulsating buckets of blood—shot a devastating hate-look at the baseball-capped kid and screamed, "Shut the fuck up! If I want your advice I'll ask for it! Who the fuck are you?" Whoa boy, what a loud yell. Dom could probably be heard all across the country from Las Vegas to Atlantic City.

Dom took his cane (he had broken his leg several months before this incident and was in the process of recovery), and I thought for sure the baseball-capped kid was about to be hammered into a baseball-capped gelatin. Thankfully, the 6'4" Stickman stepped between Dominator and the shivering, shriveling baseball-capped cringer who now, white as a ghost, ran away from the table as fast as his legs could carry him. The Five Horsemen colored up and went to get some gelato.

No doubt we do have situations at the table where we tend to be on the verge of losing our cool, or we do have situations where we actually lose it, as Dom did here. The only way to handle such situations is to train ourselves to ignore them or to leave the table before we commit murder. Either one. You actually don't want to lose your cool, because you get no benefit from doing so, and it certainly can't help your throw.

Some Rightside bettors get themselves into a snit when Darksiders are at the table. Some players become homicidal when someone puts his hands over the table or makes late bets. Other controlled shooters have apoplexy when chips are in their landing zone. Getting riled up over any of these things is counterproductive. However, if such things do rile you up and you can't get them out of your mind, then read the next chapter carefully.

CHAPTER 14

Meditation and Visualization

Meditation

Meditation can help you become a relaxed and calmly focused dice controller. Meditation can help all aspects of your game and your life. It isn't hard to learn a method of meditation that is easy to do, does not take up much time, and can actually be used at the table while you are shooting.

I will describe a simple though powerful form of meditation that can be done before, during, and after your play. It can be done daily for just its health benefits. It doesn't take long either. A simple session of just 20 minutes will achieve an alpha brain wave that means you are in a relaxed state of mental awareness.

In your home or hotel room, you can meditate with your eyes closed. When you are at the table throwing those dice, you can actually meditate with your eyes open as you go through your routine of setting the dice, gripping the dice, aiming the dice, backswinging, forward moving, and releasing the dice. By doing such meditation you will block out the casino world, and all the distractions that can occur at the table or in your mind become merely distant noises that don't affect you in any way. When you meditate properly, sounds are heard, but they are not distracting at all. They just are there. There is no work to the meditation I will teach you. You will not be forcing yourself to do it. The meditation will just happen naturally.

Please keep in mind that this meditation has nothing to do with religion. The technique you will learn helps you relax, gets your brain into an alpha state (i.e., relaxed awareness), rejuvenates you, and gives you energy to play craps in a relaxed fashion—which is what it's all about!

Here are step-by-step instructions for your meditation:

- Sit in a chair with your feet on the floor.
- Have one hand touch the other hand on your lap. You can intertwine them if you wish.
- Close your eyes.
- Take a deep breath.
- Start saying your mantra in your mind. Your mantra is the phrase "Ah-Ing."
- You do not have to say your mantra in tune to your breathing.
- Sometimes the mantra will go with your breathing, and sometimes it won't.
- Just keep repeating the mantra in your mind.
- As you get deeper into the meditative state, your head might move. It may fall down to your chest, twist from one side to the other, go back or down—this is all normal.
- You do not force the mantra—there will be times when you hear noises and your mind goes to the noise (your mantra seems to stop).
- When you realize that you are not saying the mantra in your mind, you start saying it again. No force required.
- It is normal for your mind to start listening to a noise or to start creating images, dialogues, and monologues.
- You never force yourself to relax—that can't be done. Just say your mantra in your mind when you remember to say it.
- There is no such thing as a distraction from meditation. Even if someone interrupts you and you talk to them, once that's over, you go right back to saying your mantra in your mind.
- Sometimes you will fall asleep or be in such a deep state that you will seem to be asleep—this is normal.

Can you say your mantra while you are actually playing craps? Yes, you can do this even with your eyes open. It will not be as deep a meditation, but it will keep you relaxed and focused. The world of the casino will become nothing but vague background noise off in the distance somewhere.

If you are looking for health benefits from meditation, then meditate for 20 minutes in the morning and 20 minutes in the early evening. When you are in a casino, try to meditate before a craps session if possible. If you are not staying in the hotel, find a chair in the lobby, sit, close your eyes, and do all of the aforementioned steps. It doesn't matter if people are there—many people sit in chairs with their eyes closed. You'll look normal.

Visualization

Visualization is a totally different kind of experience, as your mind must do some work to set up the parameters of what you are trying to accomplish. You will picture every aspect of your controlled throw in your mind, in real time and at times in slow motion. You will not fast-forward any part of it. You will do this exactly as you do it in the casino. You might even want to picture your favorite casino or a specific casino and place yourself in it. Maybe even place yourself at your favorite table.

Here are step-by-step instructions for your visualization:

- See the dealers, the box person, and the stick person. Look at their faces. This is real. Fill in all the aspects of the casino from your position at the craps table.
- Hear the sounds of the casino.
- See the dice in the center of table in front of the box person.
- See the dice being passed to you by the stick person. Actually watch the dice being slid along the layout to you.
- See the dice placed in front of you.
- See the stick person take away the stick from the dice.
- Pick up the dice.
- Set the dice.
- Grip the dice.
- Pick the dice up.
- Aim the dice.
- Do your gentle backswing—a perfect backswing.

- Bring the dice forward in a perfect pendulum swing (or reverse swing).
- Release the dice perfectly.
- See the dice in the air as they spin perfectly.
- See the dice bounce perfectly.
- See the dice hit the back wall perfectly.
- See the dice bounce back perfectly.
- See them land in a perfect way, showing the exact set you used when you set the dice.
- Hear the stick person's call.
- Now repeat all of the above for several turns with the dice.
- You never seven out, you just end the visualization.

Using both meditative and visualization techniques, you should improve your game in a dramatic way. Take time out every day to practice them, just as you practice your controlled throw. We have stated the following in books and articles for many years, but it bears repeating: Once you have developed a controlled throw, the game becomes 80 percent mental and 20 percent physical. Those of you who were accomplished athletes or musicians know how much of your performance takes place in your mind. In craps we sometimes call this the "rolling zone." You have to train your mind just as you train your body. To be an advanced or elite dice controller, the mind is as important as the perfect grip. So keep that in mind.

CHAPTER 15

The Casino Isn't
Your Only Problem

In the casino's deserted bathroom—usually one that was out of the way and not often used—they would come up behind a man as he stood at the urinal, grab his throat in the classic police sleeper hold, and squeeze the breath out of him. The man would fall to the floor and his wallet, rings, necklaces, and watch would be stolen from him. The thieves would walk out of the bathroom and escape into the night. Even if someone else should walk into the bathroom and see this, it rarely resulted in the person assisting the victim, for fear of his life.

A woman is not safe in the ladies bathrooms either. Some casinos have those pocketbook holders on the door or near the door inside the stall. A thief reaching inside from outside the door can easily grab the purse and disappear in a flash. This is often done even in crowded ladies rooms as it takes but a second to accomplish.

The man and wife are checking in, and a pleasant man or woman strikes up a conversation as they wait on line. His crony stands to the side of the couple and surreptitiously opens her purse and takes out her wallet. He walks away after closing her purse. No one is the wiser until the couple goes to the room and discovers that the wallet is missing.

The above three paragraphs are just preludes to the array of crimes (and other problems) you face in casino environs each and every day. Rarely are casino criminals captured, because most of the security for the casino exists to protect the casinos from cheaters, mistakes, and various types of criminals at their games. But in the bathrooms, in the lobbies, in the elevators, in the hallways, and in the rooms, there is little protection because crimes can be committed so fast that security—even if it is carefully watching these areas—doesn't have time to react.

Outside those casinos can be even worse, as violent crime manifests itself more readily out there. In the casinos a thief pummeling someone takes too much time, but out in the street or in the self-parking garages, vicious criminals can seriously hammer a victim, and they often do serious damage. In Atlantic City, in the streets and sometimes even on the usually secure Boardwalk, the scum of the earth looks to slime its way to your good fortune, often assaulting you in the process.

Casino towns such as Las Vegas and Atlantic City, indeed most casino venues, are bright lights to the ravenous moths of criminality. While we players are attracted to casinos to win money from Lady Luck's largesse, these human predators are attracted to us in order to take our money and our jewelry and perhaps our health as well.

So let's go through some of the ways the criminal enemies of the player go about their nefarious business.

1. **The Men's Room A:** In the men's room, do not stand at the urinals when doing your business. You make yourself an easy target for someone to stand behind you and choke you into unconsciousness. Use the toilet in a stall to urinate. There is usually no security in the bathroom except in those upper-echelon hotels that have a couple of bathroom attendants and/or shoe-shine setups. Don't go to the out-of-the-way bathrooms where few men go. These are great criminal lairs.

2. **The Men's Room B:** "Hey, guys, anyone want to go to the bathroom?" Yes, you hear women say this to the other women all the time, but men usually make private pilgrimages to the john. Don't. There is safety in numbers. Short of having a gun, a would-be robber isn't going to tackle two or more men. It's too dangerous for him.

3. **The Ladies Room:** The ladies rooms without attendants are easy targets too. Women and purses are an alluring combination. Don't hang your purse on those stall doors. Always hold your purse. Thankfully many casinos now have stall doors in the ladies room with the hook in the middle of the door. Short of being Elastic

Woman, few thieves can reach over and down that far. So, in these stalls it is probably safe to hang your purse.

4. **Purse Position in the Casino:** In the casino, keep your purse on your body in such a way that a criminal would have to carry you away along with your purse in order to rob you. If you play the slot machines, it is not wise to put your purse between the machines. It can be stolen from different directions if you do that. A person talks to you and you turn your head while his or her accomplice just grabs the purse and runs away. The purse can sometimes be stolen from behind the machine as well. At craps, some women will put their purse on the drink rail. Bad choice. At blackjack and other table games where you sit, wrap the purse on the chair in such a way that a thief would have to pick up the entire chair—with you in it—to get at that purse.

5. **Top Pocket:** If you carry cash, do not put it in your pants pockets. Make sure you have a shirt with a front pocket that can be securely buttoned. Put your money/wallet in there. It is usually too daring for a thief to face you and rip off your pocket to get to the money. If you have a devious sense of humor, you can stuff a cheap wallet bulging with fake bills and put it in your back pocket. When a pickpocket opens the wallet, there are the fake bills for him to curse over. Want more fun at the criminal's expense? Put some scentless powder on the bills and inform the criminal in a note that the powder is a deadly poison and he must get to the hospital's emergency room immediately or die. Okay, okay, so much for fantasizing. One last note, you should wear pants that have buttons on the pockets. It is just an added line of protection. Cargo pants fit the bill quite nicely.

6. **Credit:** In order not to carry wads of cash around the casino before playing, getting credit is a good way to go. Of course, if you win a bundle, then you have to carry your chips or credit slips to the cage.

7. **Ask for Security:** If you do win a bundle, as many dice controllers have, then do not leave the table and walk to the cage without security coming along with you. Do not go to your car without security coming with you. Do not go to your room without security coming with you. Thieves hang around the tables just looking for big winners to jump when they get a chance. In Atlantic City, one of

the Captain's best friends, Jimmy P., was tackled as he entered the elevator and had thousands stolen from him in the process.

8. **Ask for a Check:** If you have an outrageously good session and you win over $10,000, you might consider having the casino write you a check as opposed to taking cash. It is an added safety measure. Any win over $10,000 is reported to the IRS, so asking for a check is no big deal.

9. **Do Not Flash:** Everyone is happy to win big. But flashing your chips as you walk to the cage is a sign that reads, "Hey, you criminals, look how much I have won!" Put your chips in your pockets and then keep your hands in your pockets too. Ladies, you might consider wearing pants with pockets as well when you play those table games. Of course, if your pants pockets have buttons, that helps too. Then all you do is make sure your hands stay outside those pockets, preferably touching them to feel those chips as you walk to the cage.

10. **Chipping Correctly:** Check out how the casinos lay out their chips. In the center are the high-denomination chips, those worth $5,000 or more; then the next levels are on either side of those; then the $500 chips are on either side of those; then the $100 chips are on either side of those; then the $25 chips on either side of those; and so on. The chips are arranged this way so that if someone wants to reach over and steal chips, the closest chips to the thief will be the lowest denomination. When you are playing craps (or any other table game), do the exact same thing. Railbirds who attempt to scoop up some chips from you will have a much tougher time if your lowest denominations surround your high denominations.

11. **The Watchmen and Watchwomen:** No, these folks aren't the new breed of superhero; they are the individuals who stand right behind you at the tables. Most of the time they are just harmless watchers of the game, but sometimes they are criminals looking to assess how much you have won or how much you have in your rack. No one has to deal with these people. Just say to the floor person that the individual should move back as he is making you uncomfortable. If you want, you can turn around and tell the person to move back.

12. **See the Whites of Their Eyes:** I've never understood this. You think a criminal is following you so...you don't turn around to see. Do you

think the person, if he is there and if he is actually following you, will go away? Criminals don't want to be noticed. In a casino, if you think someone is following you, turn around and look him right in the eyes. Usually that is enough to make them pretend they aren't following you, and they will walk away looking for another victim. If the person seems to be of a stronger bent, then walk over to the security desk and ask to be escorted to your room. Rarely will a criminal tackle you *and* a security guard.

13. **My Kingdom for a Valet:** I once saw a video of a horrifying crime in the self-parking garage of a major casino. Several thugs jumped and almost beat to death a middle-aged man and his wife as they were opening their car. The thieves robbed them and then stole the car. From that moment on I realized that valet was the way to go. Do not be so cheap that you risk your well-being to save a few bucks. You don't want "He Never Paid for Parking" on your tombstone.

14. **Elevator Trip Not Mandatory:** You are standing waiting to get on the elevator and someone comes up to get on as well. Something about this person makes you feel uncomfortable. Most people will think, *Oh, I can't just not get on the elevator. I might hurt this person's feelings.* Nonsense. If you experience the least feeling of discomfort, *do not* get on the elevator. Now what if the person who makes you feel uncomfortable gets on the elevator when you are all alone and in the elevator already? Walk out. If other people are on the elevator, get off when the first person gets off and wait for another elevator. Do not allow yourself to ever be alone on an elevator with someone who makes you feel uncomfortable.

15. **Wallflower:** Once you are in an elevator, try to stand against the back wall or the side walls with your back to the wall. That gives you a good view of everyone on the elevator.

16. **Bump and Grab:** If someone bumps you, immediately put your hand to your money. Men, that means grab your wallet and women hold on to that purse with a death grip.

17. **Never Yell "Help!" in a Hallway:** So the guy is about to jump you in the hallway or he has jumped you. If you scream out "Help!" or "Help me!" the likelihood is that no one will fling open their door and come storming into the hallway to rescue you. You'd be lucky

if someone even bothered to call security and if they did, you'd be lucky if security arrived within 10 minutes. So how do you get help? Yell, "Fire! Fire! Fire" as loud as you can. Every door on the floor will open, and some people will actually run into the hallway. Good chance the criminal will get out of there. With many people viewing the situation, there is more pressure for them to at least call for security so they don't look like total cowards by not doing so.

18. **Knock, Knock:** The guy is trailing you in the hallway. So start knocking on the doors as you head for your room. Some people will open the doors. If you can get someone to take you in, you are safe. If not, tell the person to call security. Or say you don't remember what room you and your friends/family are in. And always make it sound as if you have a lot of people with you. That might discourage the person from attacking you since there are witnesses.

19. **I'm With Security:** This is a version of the home invasion. You hear the knock on your room door and look out the keyhole. The person you see claims he is with security. Sometimes the person is, and there are some times when the person isn't; he is merely waiting for you to open the door so he can pounce. Just tell him you are calling down to security to confirm it. The criminal will leave. If he is a security agent, he will stay. Of course, make the call and determine the truth of the situation. Ask the security people why the man has come up. Then ask the security agent why he has come up. If the stories are the same, he is from security.

20. **Key Check Bad Bet:** Many hotels have key-check personnel as you enter the elevator areas. This is to make sure that only people with keys are allowed in. That's great, but getting a key to a room is no hard feat to accomplish. Just about anyone can get one. So while these checkpoints might help a little, don't trust them to keep you safe. Your eyes and ears and brain are your best protection.

21. **Criminals Usually Look Like Criminals:** We aren't talking Armani-suited Wall Street scammers here. We are talking street crime of the indoor variety, and street criminals usually look like street criminals. If you notice someone who looks like a criminal, then figure that he or she is a criminal. If you think you are being watched by this person, then go to the security desk or to a security guard and strike

up a conversation. Remember that criminals aren't looking to get caught, and they will usually go after other game of which there is plenty in the casino.

22. **Don't Look Well-Off:** Two people are walking by the thief. One wears expensive clothes, has real gold jewelry on his wrist and dangling from his neck, and wears an expensive watch to boot. His shoes are made from the Golden Fleece. The second person wears cheap clothes—maybe a sweatsuit, sneakers, or cargo pants and a cheap shirt. His watch probably cost about $29.99. Who is the thief going after? Unless this thug is even dumber than the dumbest of the dumb, he'll eye the wealthy-looking gentleman. Playing craps in a casino is not a fashion show, so dress down even if you are a high roller. This holds true for women too. Be comfortable but underdressed. Clothing is the billboard of a person's wealth, and thieves are billboard readers.

23. **Safe and Sound:** If your room has a safe, use it. Put your jewelry, your money, most of your credit cards, your medicines, and other valuables in it. If the casino hotel does not have safes in the rooms, then open a safe deposit box at the main desk.

24. **Traveler's Checks:** So you don't want to carry cash and you don't want to get credit. Then the best thing to do is bring traveler's checks to the casino and cash what you need for your upcoming session of play. Don't cash any more than that.

25. **Be Aware of the Chip Grabbers:** When you are playing craps you must be aware of every bet you have on the table and watch as the dealers pay off the bets. Sometimes grabbers will reach over and take your win if you aren't watching. Often this will happen by accident, but there are some pretty slick players out there who will snatch your win and keep it if you don't notice what has just happened.

26. **The Male Ego:** She is beautiful or maybe not so beautiful, seductive or maybe not so seductive, but she takes an instant interest in you. She looks enamored of you. She talks to you and expresses much appreciation for your sense of humor (even if you are a dullard), your looks (even if you are ugly), and your betting size (as long as it is big). Obviously, the woman is either a hooker or a crook. You

aren't irresistible. That is the garbage that is sold on commercials. Aside from the fact that this woman might give you a serious disease to bring home with you, she will also "dismoney" you as well. She might also have her male counterpart mug you.

27. **I Lost My Key:** Some ladies of the night (and mornings and afternoons) will stand near the elevator banks where high rollers have to use their keys in the elevator lock to get to the comped high-roller suites. They will ask to go with you. Not a good idea. Two things can happen. They can mug you or they can indeed go to your room with you and then two more things might happen in your room. They can have sex with you for a steep fee or they can drug you and take your money, leaving you passed out and perhaps injured.

28. **Walk or Don't Walk:** If you are in an unfamiliar casino town and you like to take walks, then make sure you ask the concierge or a dealer or a security person if it is safe to take a walk outside. Make sure you know which streets are safe and which have steely-eyed lowlifes hanging out on them looking to cause trouble. The beautiful AP and I have had several encounters with criminals when we walked in the wrong areas of unfamiliar towns. We escaped, but such incidents are frightening.

29. **Drink Down:** If someone spills a drink while you are playing, you can dry your clothes off later. Grab your chips or hold your hands over your chip rack! One of the oldest scams in the book is to drop a drink, and as everyone is leaping out of the way, the drink spiller scoops up some of a player's chips from his rack. When a drink spills over the layout, everyone looks at the event including the box person, the dealers, and the players. It is a great time for the railbird to snatch a few chips from the rail.

30. **Count Your Chips Before You Color Up:** Before you lay down your chips to color up after your play, make sure you know exactly how much money you have there. Divide your chips by color and hand them in this way. There is no rush in coloring up; do it methodically and correctly. As good as they are, box people and dealers can add up your chips incorrectly. If you know exactly how much you have, you can correct any mistakes. Never take your eyes off your chips as

the box person or dealer is counting them. The box person or dealer is not looking to cheat you, but mistakes are made, so be watchful.

31. **My System Works, and It Is Free:** One of the oldest scams in casino gambling, a scam even some advantage players might fall into, involves the scammer giving his system away for free. The only catch is that he will come to the casino with you and the two of you will share in your profits. A lot of people fall for this one. The player invests the money, and if he loses, he loses all of it. The scammer does not share in the loss. But if the player wins, the scammer gets a percentage, usually half, of the player's win.

32. **Weird and Wacky Dice-Control Teachings:** Since the Captain discovered and explained how to use a controlled throw at craps, many shadowy figures have pretended to understand and execute his methods. These frauds have developed a variety of useless throws that don't work but do work to make the scammer quite a bit of dough. Some individuals of lesser talent but of honest motivation have also attempted to teach students how to control the dice, often with eccentric throws that do not work or do not work as well as the Captain's throw. You will note that some of these poor souls are dismissive of the Captain for a variety of silly, uninformed, and unfounded reasons. Some are positively nasty individuals who feel the need to build themselves up by knocking their clear superiors down. Be that as it may, be careful of whom you ask for advice concerning how to control the dice. Wrong teaching can cost you a lot of money.

33. **Trend-Betting Systems:** Again, even advantage players can sometimes fall for trend-betting systems usually developed by individuals who claim to be PhDs or physicists or engineers, who articulate a whole bunch of mathematical gobbledygook that proves what happened in the past will or will not happen in the immediate future. I have seen some controlled shooters fall for these schemes with sad results. Again, no trend-betting system works at a random game.

34. **Germs Love You:** Yes, there are elements you face that you can't see, but they are everywhere around you: germs and viruses. Your hotel room is loaded with them. Your remote, your telephone, and

the door handle to your room are the best places for germs to lounge while waiting for your unsuspecting fingers to touch them, then touch your eyes or nose, and then enter your body to give you something other than money to take home with you. When you first get into your room, take out an alcohol rub and wipe the remote, the telephone, and the door handle, inside and out.

35. **Chip Germs:** You are playing craps and several players are coughing or sneezing. They are then touching their chips. Their germs are hopping onto the chips, waiting to give you a dose of your fellow player's disease-infested body. Of course, casinos will not let you wash down your chips as you are playing, but you can take the precaution of not putting your hands to your face as you play. Germs get into your body usually through your tear ducts. When you are playing, you can also wipe your hands with alcohol rubs. If you play the slots or any other machine, wipe the *play* and *hold* buttons before you touch them.

36. **Clean Those Cups and Glasses:** In your hotel room, your cups and drinking glasses probably look clean as clean can be. Unfortunately, sometimes this is an illusion because they have been cleaned not with soap and water but with glass cleaner, something that is obviously not healthy for you. So before you use any cups or glasses in your room, wash them out thoroughly. The same applies to coffee makers and any silverware in the rooms.

37. **Check for Bedbugs:** Telltale signs of bedbugs are usually lines of dirt on the bottom sheet. Check your sheets before you put your body in bed, unless you want to sleep with the insects of the night. Bringing bedbugs home is a horrible thing. They are extremely difficult to get rid of once they are in your home.

38. **Close to the Driver:** In many casino towns, the best mode of transportation might be buses or jitneys. If so, then on nearly deserted buses or jitneys, sit as close to the bus driver as you can. Jitneys are targeted by thieves because some think the people riding those jitneys have money on them to gamble with.

39. **Don't Share Cabs:** This goes without saying. You can be a clear mark in a cab. There's nowhere to run and nowhere to hide, and the cab driver is probably not going to risk his safety to protect yours. If

someone hops into a cab with you, open the door and tell the cab driver you don't share rides. If he doesn't respond as you would like, get out of the cab.

40. **Don't Give Credit-Card Information Over the Phone:** You've checked into your room and are getting settled. The phone rings, and a voice on the line says, "Sorry to bother you. This is Wendy from the front desk, and we must have taken your credit-card information incorrectly. Can you please give it to us again?" Many people give the requested information. Don't do this. Tell the person on the line you'll come downstairs to let them run your card again. This scam has been used in many hotels. Never give your credit-card numbers over the phone!

CHAPTER 16

Take Them for All They're Worth

I t was a glorious afternoon in May in an off-strip Las Vegas casino. After three happy days of Dom and me hammering this casino in blackjack, with our betting spreads going from one unit in low counts (house-favorable counts) up to 10 units in high counts (player-favorable counts), this double-deck game with great rules had been ours from the get-go. There was no heat either; none of the pit personnel had even bothered us. They laughed and joked with us, as did the dealers. Everyone had been super friendly from the moment we stepped into the casino and played our first session.

Also, Dominator and I were the only ones who ever tipped the blackjack and craps dealers, so our action was great for them too. I didn't think anyone at this casino knew who we were, even though we were handing in our player's cards and getting RFB (full comp) for everything—gourmet meals, beautiful suites, limo rides wherever we wished to go, shows, and even airfare; in short, the casino gave us the real *Life of Reilly*.

Our good fortune was the same in craps. While neither of us had any monster rolls to this point, that fact really didn't matter. We had consistently won on our rolls in the teens, hitting repeating number after repeating number. Indeed, we had won on even shorter rolls in the single digits. On-axis shooters don't need monster rolls to bring home the bacon; we just need to consistently hit the same numbers over and over and over again.

Still, monster rolls are fun, and they are the stuff of big bragging in voice and print. I don't mind bragging either. It is fun if what you have to brag about actually happened, preferably in front of witnesses. When lightning strikes, it's certainly remarkable.

And that afternoon lightning struck. Dominator and I got so hot at the craps table that we could have burned down Chicago had Mrs. O'Leary's cow not done it before us. Two of our students happened to come to the table at the start of Dom's first turn with the dice. That was strange, since we had rarely met anyone we knew at this particular casino—one of the reasons we went there, in addition to its great games. I nodded to them; they nodded to me and bought in. Each took a position at the end of the table to my left as I was on SL1.

With the addition of these two students, the table had seven of us altogether—the two students and three others who were obviously locals. Dom was on SR1. Dom was passed the dice and proceeded to roll a masterful 23, a really nice, money-making hand from the world's greatest dice controller. I rolled an eight hand—with four 6s and one 8 before I sevened out, a short but winning hand.

The dice went around the table. The two students were out of their shooting positions since Dom and I each had one of the locals next to us at SR2 and SL2. So the students did not shoot that afternoon but passed the dice when it was their turn. The locals did shoot. The local next to me went next and had a nice hand of 18, winging the dice down the table as if he wanted them to go through the back wall. I got on his roll after the 5-Count and bet one Come bet on him. I won several of these, and when he sevened out I had a profit from his roll. The man clapped for himself after his roll and so did the rest of us. This guy was a slender, good-looking man of about 70 with wispy white hair who was neatly dressed as if he were going to play golf later that afternoon. So I thought of him as the Golfer.

"Nice roll," I said to him.

"Thanks," he said.

In our dice-control classes I always tell controlled shooters to act like regular craps players at the table. If a shooter makes his point, clap; if the shooter hits numbers, clap. Don't talk to the shooter, don't pat him on the back, don't bother him in any way, but certainly clap and cheer.

Dom and I do this because that is what craps players do. The worst thing you can do at a craps table is attempt to look professional. Look professional at work, but look as if you are having fun at a game people play for fun. That's common sense. When the roll is over and if you've made some money, congratulate the shooter on a fine performance, which contributes to the camaraderie at the table.

Our two students passed up the dice, and the local at the end of the table on Dom's side went next. It was early afternoon, but this tall, strapping, beer-bellied man of about 50, who had seen far better days and was a little tipsy at this point (he would get far more "tipsy" as the session progressed) was unshaven with several days' growth on his face. He wore a stained, faded T-shirt of some football team I have since forgotten. His fingernails were dirty too, which I took to mean he worked with his hands—or he was a pig—and his nose had tufts of hair sprouting out of his nostrils and ears. In fact, I did think of him as the Pig.

The Pig got the dice, and he was one of those players who liked to bounce the dice off the wall under him until the faces he wanted appeared. When these faces finally appeared (sometimes after several months), he set the dice—which also took about half a year—and then he threw those dice high into the air. Several times the stick person had to tell him to lower his arc because the dice were going above the stick person's eye level, which is a no-no in craps since the stick person has to watch the dice and the bets in the center of the table as the dice are in the air. He can't do that if the dice are over his head.

The Pig sevened out just after establishing his point. He snorted and ordered a beer from the cocktail waitress. Since the casino was not crowded, the cocktail server, a pretty young lady whose weathered face had hosted too many tans and inhaled too many cigarettes, was always hovering nearby. The Pig never tipped. He would just take his beer, gulp some, ignore the server, put the beer in the drink rack under the chip rack, and continue playing and occasionally burping and scratching his crotch.

The local standing next to Dom on his right shot next. He was a young man, really skinny, timid, mousy-eyed, seemingly muscleless, displaying a somewhat puffy hairdo with a trace of slow balding, and he was quite,

quite pale. He really didn't look very healthy, and his mannerisms also seemed a little fussy. Dom had whispered to me when the young man was buying in that he thought the guy was gay. The guy also looked as if he were several minutes away from dying. I thought of him as the Dying One. The Pig constantly looked at him with a combination of disdain and disgust.

The Dying One took the dice and gently threw them down the table. His throw actually looked pretty good, very soft, although he was not a controlled shooter. On the Dying One's very first throw, the Pig slobbered, "You throw like a girl. Be manly. Christ almighty."

"I *am* a *girl*," said the Dying One, her voice dripping with sarcasm, shooting the Pig a look that could turn him into bacon, well-done and extra crispy. The Pig's eyes bulged a little, his face turned pinkish under his whiskers, he snorted, looked down, grabbed his crotch and then his beer, and gulped the rest of it down his throat.

"Another beer, sister," he said to the cocktail waitress in an overly manly voice.

The Dying One made it past the 5-Count and then immediately sevened out. I made money because she sevened out just as I put down a Come bet.

It was now Dom's second turn with the dice. His eyes had that fiery look. I think the Pig had irritated him when he got on the girl who we thought was a gay guy. Now Dom is no PC overly sensitive type when it comes to sexual orientation, race, ethnicity, or whatever other labels the PC crowd catalogs people under to separate them from everyone else. He treats everyone equally, and that can be good or bad for that person. That's just Dom. But he does have class, whereas the Pig was classless. The Pig had gotten under Dom's skin. It's not too hard to get under Dom's skin. Those who have met Dom, played with us, or taken our classes know this about him. He can be volatile.

Also the Pig dressed like a pig. Dom is a meticulous dresser with a clothes closet in his house as big as some people's living rooms. I think the only person Dom has ever been able to tolerate who doesn't dress up and looks to be somewhat ratty is me. I've never been a clothes horse. My clothes closet is about four feet by two feet and is half full of clothes I rarely wear. Give me sweats or give me death.

Now Dom's eyes were burning, and he had a slight scowl on his face. I like that fiery look in Dom's eyes. I like that tiny little scowl too. Yes, he does sometimes seem insane when that look and scowl appear, but they often herald a great roll from the world's greatest dice master.

And so it went. Dom took the dice, set the dice, rolled the dice, and off we went to the races for a spectacular hour-long roll of 63 numbers. He was almost perfect in his throw, totally on axis on a healthy majority of them. He was making his usual array of bets, including hopping some doubles such as 3:3. Dom really likes to hop his numbers on the come-out roll where the only thing in his mind is that Hop bet.

Naturally I could see those two students of ours quizzically looking at him when he put his money on those Hop bets. They looked at me too. I whispered, "I'll explain later." This scenario happens almost all the time when students are at the table with Dom.

The Pig was happily wallowing in his slop too. Cheering and drinking and burping, he spewed beer-saturated saliva over the layout as he roared his approval as Dom hit number after number. I think the Pig's disgusting antics spurred Dom on even more. The whites of Dom's eyes were actually red, the way Christopher Lee's eyes were blood red when he played Dracula in various horror movies such as *Horror of Dracula*.

When Dom progresses in one his monster rolls, he starts to get angry. He looks at the dice as if he hates them. Maybe they talk to him, say nasty things to him—I don't know. I've written about this before. Unlike most craps players who find that super-long monster rolls make them happy, Dom just keeps getting angrier and angrier as the roll progresses. It might have to do with the fact that he knows somewhere deep down in his subconscious that sooner or later the damn 7 will roll and gets pissed beforehand because of that. Then, when the 7 does show, he storms off and kicks a slot machine. Shorter rolls in the teens and 20s do not have this effect on him, but once he starts getting into monster territory, he slowly transforms into a monster himself.

I don't actually remember Dom's roll moment by moment because I was fascinated by the Pig's spit sailing up over the layout and then falling down onto it. On occasion some droplets of his spew would hit the Dying One, who threw him looks that she probably hoped would kill him. Unfortunately, he lived.

Dom was in the rolling zone and had forgotten that the Pig even existed. He was hitting a decent proportion of his Hop bets and seemed to be truly honed in. He was in his zone, and the money poured in.

Every time he made his point, I would clap and cheer and say, "Keep it going, baby! Keep it going!" He kept it going too.

The Golfer was having fun. "Man, this guy is a great shooter!" The students were nodding their heads. This was the first time these two had ever been at a table with us, and they were seeing Dominator put on a show. And when these rolls go on, Dom starts a routine of sometimes playing an air guitar, sometimes mimicking a fishing experience he once had with a salmon that was about 10 pounds when he caught it but has now become over 30 pounds when he tells the story (20 years from now the creature will be whale-sized), and sometimes Dom just talks to the dice. When a throw is a little off, he'll shout out, "Give me some luck!" That shout is to ward off the 7 because he feels his shot was random. As you know, not every controlled shooter's throw is controlled during an extended run.

Interestingly enough, except for Dom and me, the other players were basically red-chip players, although the Dying One and the Pig did begin to increase their bets as Dom's roll continued.

When Dom sevened out, the table exploded with applause. Dom walked away, ignoring the applause, found a slot machine nearby, and kicked it. The Pig, now with drool on his chin, said, "Whas the fuck's wrung wit das jer-p?" He couldn't quite finish his sentence because he burped on the last word which I believe he wanted to be "jerk" but instead came out "jer-p." We all looked at the Pig. How could he criticize a guy who just rolled a 63?

"What a roll," said the Golfer.

"He rolled 63 numbers," I said. I keep track of the number of rolls by using my chips. Rolls one through four are white chips ($1). When it reaches five, I use one red chip. Six through nine are one red and white chips. Ten will be two reds, and on up the chip ladder I go. When the Captain rolled his 147-number hand, I had a black chip ($100) in my count pile. That was the first and only time I used black in all the years I have been playing craps.

"Wow!" said the Golfer.

Dom returned to the table. As he tells the story in all of our dice-control classes, he said to me, "Okay, Frank, do me better. I know you will do me better," and then I had the roll of a lifetime.

Well, yes, he did say that, but on my turn I didn't have the roll of a lifetime. I rolled a 12 and sevened out. The Golfer passed the dice, and so did the two students. Everyone wanted Dominator to shoot again, except for the Pig, who took the dice and did his thing. But he was wrecked by this point and couldn't quite remember what faces of the dice were appearing as he banged them against the wall under him. Finally the box person said, "Sir, just pick the dice up and throw them. We don't have all day."

The Pig started to argue, and I walked to the bathroom. When I got back, the Pig was arguing about something else. I looked down at the table and it was wet. This disgusting "icr p" had spilled his beer on the table. The cocktail waitress came over and soaked a towel with the guy's beer.

"Suster giip ee anotter wahn," slurred the Pig.

"Is he still rolling?" I asked the Golfer.

"No, he sevened out and then dumped the remains of his beer on the table. He's sloshed."

After the Pig's place was cleaned up, Dominator got the dice, as the Dying One had also passed up her turn. He had a good roll of 18 with a lot of 6s and 8s. Now it was my turn again.

"Go, go Frank, go for it!" shouted Dominator. The Pig snorted and rasped, "I ga piss nah. Dis eye cont shoo." He weaved his way toward the bathroom.

"What a fucking dick," said Dom.

"What did he say?" asked one of the students.

"He said Frank can't shoot the dice, something like that," said the other student.

"Shooter's got the dice!" shouted the stick person.

You know, in some turns with the dice totally disparate thoughts come into your head. Usually when this happens they whip by your consciousness and disappear into the blackness of thoughts thought and gone and never to be remembered. But I often tend to catch these and remember them. A passing thought crossed my mind: *Dom had a 63 roll and no one came to the table to join us. This place is really dead.*

I had $25 on the Pass Line. I set the dice in the All-Sevens set, established a point of 9, and took the full 4X Odds. I placed the 6 and 8 for $150 each, but I hesitated to bet any Hop bets because I knew the students had already been stunned by Dominator's betting them. I should have bet Hop bets, but I just couldn't do it. A passing thought: *I have to give my usual obfuscating explanation of why Dom makes Hop bets when I finish this session. I don't look forward to that.* You just don't want novice and intermediate dice controllers to imitate elite ones such as Dominator.

I set the dice in the 3V. That is my favorite set, and I have been using it throughout my dice-playing career. Some players have actually nicknamed me "Mr. 3V." I gripped carefully, aimed the dice, and threw them softly into the air, where they backspun their way to the back wall.

Passing thought: *There are plenty of slot machines being played, just no table-game players.*

The stick person called out, "Six the hard way!"

Dominator yelled, "Keep hitting those hard sixes!" He collected a stack of chips.

I set the dice.

Passing thought: *This is definitely a slot place during the week.*

I throw.

One of the students said, "Yes! Another!"

I set the dice. The Dying One just bet the 6 for $30. I throw.

The Golfer said, "Three hard sixes in a row!"

I set the dice.

Passing thought: *The Pig's area is dry. I don't feel wetness on the dice when I get them back.*

I throw.

"Just 6s and 8s," shouts Dom. "Just 6s and 8s!"

I set the dice. I throw the dice.

"Nine, nina nine!" shouts the dealer. I made my point.

Passing thought: *I like this casino. I like the table crew. The stick person steps back to give me a clear view to the back wall.* Why not? Dom and I both have money on the table for the dealers. They are in the game too. We always keep the dealers in the game.

I set the dice. I throw. Point of 6 established.

I set the dice. I throw.

"Six, right back with it, a repeater, easy six!" shouts the stick person.

"Hop the hard six," says Dom, throwing out a green chip.

Passing thought: *Don't look at the students. I'm sure Dom has stunned them again.*

I set the dice. I throw. "Eight is the point!" shouts the stick person. The Dying One places the 8 for $30 and claps her hands.

I buy the 4 and 10 for $50 each. The vig is paid on a win only, so this is a good bet with a 1.3 percent house edge.

Passing thought: *She's actually not a bad-looking girl. I guess early twenties. Wound up though. Wouldn't want her dating either of my sons.*

I set. I throw.

One of the students shouts, "He owns the hard six!"

I set. I throw a garbage number.

Passing thought: *Any number I'm not on is a garbage number.*

I set. I throw a good number. I set. I throw a good number. I set. I throw a good number. I set. I throw a good number. I set. I throw a good number. I set. I throw a good number. Good numbers are any numbers I am on.

I set. I throw an 8. Made my point again.

"Same good shooter," says the stick person passing the dice to me.

Passing thought: *Oh, shit.*

The Pig is staggering back to the table. He takes off the towel the crew put over his chips and blows his nose in it and flings it to the dealer on his right. The dealer jumps out of its way and the towel falls to the floor.

"What a fucking pig," says Dominator into the casino air.

I get the dice, set the dice, throw the dice.

"Moe bee," slurs the Pig.

My new point is a 5.

"We think you have had enough, sir," says the floor person, who has been closely watching the game.

"Ah wahn bee," says the Pig. "Ah wahn bee."

I am distracted. Do I set and throw? I am not in my zone. This will be strictly random. I pause and think of my mantra. No good. My mind is on the Pig.

Passing thought: *Hit him with the dice.*

I set the dice.

Passing thought: *He might come at you.*

I grip the dice.

Passing thought: *He can hardly walk.*

I aim the dice.

Passing thought: *For God and country!*

I wing the dice at the Pig's chest. They zoom through the air like two bullets. One die skims off his shoulder and goes zooming off under the closed craps table behind us. He doesn't even notice it. The other die hits him square in that shoulder. He doesn't notice that one either.

"Same dice," I say. The dealers are grinning. The floor person scurries off to get the die that sailed off the Pig's shoulder and is now resting under the table behind us.

"Gif mee a cig rat," he says to Dom, who is taking a cigarette out of his full pack.

"I ran out," says Dom coolly. The Pig is trying to figure out—I'm guessing here—how Dom could have run out when he has a full pack in his hand.

I get the dice back. I am far more relaxed as I set the dice. I now aim. I start my backswing. The Pig drops a handful of chips all over the layout and reaches over to pick them up, dropping still more from his hand onto the layout and knocking chips off his chip rack, which fall to the floor as he pulls back his arm. I put the dice down.

The floor person walks around the table to the Pig. "I think you should take a break, sir." The Pig is having trouble picking up his chips. His hands don't seem to be obeying him. The floor person nods to the dealer, and the dealer helps the Pig pick up his chips off the layout. The floor person picks up the chips off the floor. A really big stony-faced heavily muscled security guard comes up and stands next to the Pig. This security guard could have been the Incredible Hulk if he were green.

The floor person says, "Let's cash in your chips at the cage, sir, and you take a break for a while." This floor person is quite professional.

The Pig seems about to object and then he sees the Hulk next to him and instead allows himself to be escorted to the cage by the floor person and the Hulk.

"Thank God he's gone," says the Dying One.

Dom blows out a stream of smoke. "It would have been fun to put my cigarette out in his eye." Everyone stares at Dom. A pause. Then he laughs and we all laugh. The tension created by the Pig is now dissipated.

"Okay, let's get back to the game," says the box person.

And we get back to the game.

"Come on, Frank, roll for a month," says Dom, taking a long drag from his cigarette and blowing the smoke into the air. I really wish Dom would quit smoking.

I set. I throw. And eternity happens. Well, actually, the craps equivalent of eternity. I have my best roll to that point in my career—89 numbers before I seven out.

When you have long rolls, there comes a time when you are in a dream world, an alternate universe. Your body is doing what you have trained it to do. It is operating automatically. Everything feels removed from everything else. Yes, you are there at the craps table, but you are also somewhere else far, far away. Time expands. My passing thoughts now just pass through, and I have little memory of them.

I have bits and pieces of thoughts; nothing really solid, just shimmers of what must have passed through my mind during that roll. I hear the numbers being called out by the stick person. I see several stick changes. I'm on every number by the end of the roll. I know that. The money doesn't even seem real. I don't even think anything of the money. There are just piles of chips on the numbers, just piles of chips.

I have some very big bets out there. Dom's been hopping bets like crazy, and I know he is winning many of these because he whoops it up when he does. But all of these things are in the distance, just beyond concrete reality, which is also in some distant place. It's all ephemeral and then...

"Seven! Seven out!" shouts the stick person. "What a great roll, Frank, great roll!"

I'm back in the world. The other players are clapping and cheering.

Dom walks behind the stick person to me and pats me on the back.

"Not bad," I say.

Dom laughs and hugs me. "Not bad at all! But couldn't you have gotten to a hundred?"

We color up. The Hulk walks us to the cage. I ask for a check. I don't like carrying around a lot of cash.

One of the students comes up to me. "Great roll," he says.

"Thanks," I say.

"I just wanted to ask you a question," he says.

"Dom makes those bets because he still has a little gambler left inside him. Nobody's perfect," I say.

It's now late afternoon, and I am tired and happy.

"Let's go to the pool," I say to Dom.

"No, no, I'm hot," he says. "I'm going to play some blackjack."

"Dom," I say, "you never want to quit."

"I'll play a little and then I'll meet you at the pool in an hour or so. We're having dinner at seven. We have plenty of time."

At the pool, I swim a little, take a comfortable chair, and stretch out in the shade. I'm not into sunbathing, but I do enjoy lounging by the pool. I really like this pool. There's almost no one here. The property is quite nice, but it seems to be underused during the week.

I feel a nudge on my arm. "Frank, Frank, wake up," says Dom.

"Oh man, I fell asleep. I was gone."

"All that excitement," says Dom.

He isn't happy.

"You don't look happy," I say. "You lose in blackjack?"

"I won," he says.

"Great, what a great day."

"And I've been banned," he adds.

"What?"

"Yeah, can you believe it? Those fucks banned me." (My wife, the beautiful AP, tells me to get rid of all of the "fucks" in my books when Dom speaks—except Dom owns a franchise in that word. It's how he speaks. You want to hear Dom's voice? Then "fuck" is the word! Sorry if that offends you.)

"You were banned at blackjack?"

"No, they told me I couldn't play craps or blackjack in their casino again and if I tried I'd be trespassed." Being trespassed is a serious thing because that means the casino will consider your very appearance on their property to be an illegal act of trespassing. They can't have you arrested for controlling the dice or counting cards since neither is illegal, but they can stop you from playing. But if they tell you that they no longer will allow you on their property, then the next time you show up, they can have you arrested. You are being arrested for trespassing not for skill in gambling. It is immoral, I agree, but it is the law. Casinos are private businesses, and in Las Vegas and most other states, they can ban you and/or trespass you, and that is all there is to it. Sadly, Dom and I have been trespassed in some casinos and in one whole state!

"They've been so nice," I said. "It's hard to believe they banned you."

"And you," he said.

"Me? I was here sleeping."

"They told me that when you came back into the casino they would tell you the same thing."

"Today was too much for them," I said.

"What are we supposed to do? Give them some of their money back?"

"You know what we won is really only a tiny drop in the bucket. But they want every drop in the bucket."

"Greedy fucks," said Dom, taking out his cigarettes.

"Dom, I really wish you'd stop smoking."

"I'll stop smoking when the casinos stop being greedy fucks," he said and lit up.

I guess Dom will never stop smoking.

APPENDIX I

The Captain's 5-Count

How do you position yourself to take advantage of hot rolls without losing a fortune betting on every single shooter and every single roll of the dice? How do you get the same amount or more in comps with less risk? The legendary Captain from Atlantic City developed a method called the 5-Count, which takes both these questions into consideration.

On our site, www.goldentouchcraps.com, is an interesting article discussing what the 5-Count can and can't do for smart craps players. One of our Five Horsemen, Skinny, has done a series of articles on the strength of the 5-Count, using University of Massachusetts mathematician Dr. Don Catlin's study of the 5-Count as his basis. The 5-Count cannot magically transform random rollers into controlled shooters—nothing can do that but practicing how to control the dice—but the 5-Count can find controlled shooters better than any other method, if those shooters are at your table. The only method better than the 5-Count is to know who the controlled shooter is in advance!

When the brilliant Captain was discovering his great 5-Count playing method, he knew he had three imperatives:

1. Reduce the number of random rolls you bet on to save your money;
2. Increase the likelihood that the shooters you do bet on will win you money;
3. Increase your comps based on *body time* as opposed to *risk time*.

The 5-Count accomplishes all three of the Captain's imperatives based on Dr. Catlin's study.

1. It eliminates almost 57 percent of the random rolls. You will be betting on only about 43 percent of the random rolls.
2. It gets you on the controlled shooters (the Captain called such players *rhythmic rollers*) at a higher frequency than *bet-all* players. If there is a controlled shooter at the table, you will be on him with the 5-Count 11 percent more often than bet-all players.
3. It increases comp value because of body time. You are usually given credit for 100 percent of the time you are at the table, but you are risking your money only 43 percent of the time. Indeed, you can get a *monetary edge* by betting this way. That means even against random rollers, with your small losses subtracted from your comps, you might still be ahead of the casino. The 5-Count also makes you look just like all those players who wait for some qualifying event to enter the game.

So what is the 5-Count? It is the method we use to decide which rollers to bet on. It starts with a Point number on the Come-Out roll (4, 5, 6, 8, 9, or 10) and ends with a Point/Box number. Throws between rolls No. 1 and No. 5 can be any number, except if the shooter sevens-out. Let's take a look at the various scenarios:

Example One: The Basics

Shooter's Roll #	Number Rolled	Count	Bet
1	7	0-count	0
2	*4	1-count	0
3	11	2-count	0
4	6	3-count	0
5	3	4-count	0
6	*8	5-Count	Betting begins

Example one is the bare-bones 5-Count. The shooter is on the Come-Out roll and rolls a 7, which is a winner but is not the start of the 5-Count because it isn't a Point number. (Remember that Point numbers are also called Box numbers.) His second roll is a 4. The 4 is a Point/Box number and is also his Point. Now he rolls an 11, the 2-count; then a 6, the 3-count; then a 3, the 4-count; and then an 8, another Point/Box number, which completes the 5-Count.

Example Two: The Holding Pattern

Shooter's Roll #	Number rolled	Count	Bet
1	11	0-count	0
2	7	0-count	0
3	*6	1 count	0
4	5	2-count	0
5	9	3-count	0
6	11	4-count	0
7	3	4-count and holding	0
8	2	4-count and holding	0
9	*10	5-Count	Betting begins

Example Two shows what happens when other than Point/Box numbers are thrown after the 4-count. This causes a *holding pattern*. Roll six, which was an 11, established the 4-count, but then the shooter rolled a 3 and then a 2—both of which are not Point/Box numbers—which causes the 5-Count not to be completed. The 4-count is holding until a Point/Box number is rolled. Finally, the shooter rolls a 10, which is a Point/Box number, and the 5-Count is completed.

Example Three: Shooter Makes Point

Shooter's Roll #	Number Rolled	Count	Bet
1	4	1-count	0
2	3	2-count	0
3	4 (point!)	3-count	0
4	7	4-count	0

Shooter's Roll #	Number Rolled	Count	Bet
5	11	4-count and holding	0
6	7	4-count and holding	0
7	11	4-count and holding	0
8	3	4-count and holding	0
9	*9	5-Count	Betting begins

Example Three shows what happens when a shooter actually makes his Point during the establishment of the 5-Count. His first roll is a 4, the 1-count; his second roll is a 3, the 2-count; and on his third roll he hits his Point, the 4, which is the 3-count. Now he is on the Come-Out again. He rolls a 7. Because it is a Come-Out roll, that 7 becomes the 4-count. Now the shooter rolls a string of non-Point/Box numbers (the 11, 7, 11, 3) before he finally hits another Point/Box number, the 9. The 5-Count is now completed.

How to Bet with the 5-Count

Now that you know how the 5-Count works, you have to decide how you are going to structure your betting. Remember that the 5-Count is the Captain's way to eliminate approximately six out of every 10 random rolls and save you a bundle of money. So how do we bet on the shooters who get through the 5-Count?

The best way is to make minimal Come bets and take the full Odds. The Odds bet is a wash between the casino and the player. If you can afford to take the Odds, do so—if you are a frequent player, the Odds bet will wind up being an even proposition between you and the casino.

> **Please Note:** *Dice controllers should consider always taking Odds even on random rollers, because taking Odds makes you look like a regular player. Very few Lightside players don't take the Odds.*

If you go up on three Come bets of $10 each, your risk is 1.4 percent of $30, or 42 cents.

So here is one example of how to use the Come bets in our most conservative way. You will put up a Come bet after the 5-Count is completed. This placement is favorable to you because there are eight ways to win on the initial placement of the Come bet (7 and 11) and only four ways to lose (2, 3, and 12). You have a 2-to-1 edge on this placement. If the shooter makes a Point number, your bet goes up on the number, and you take Odds.

Now you place another Come bet *if you wish*. If the shooter sevens-out, you lose the bet on the number and win the bet just placed on the Come. If he rolls another Box number you go up on that number if you wish and take the Odds. If you wish to go up on a third number, you simply put out another Come bet. If the shooter has actually made his Point, then you make a Pass Line bet. We will use $10 betting units. You can translate these into your betting units.

Example Four: Come Betting

Shooter's Roll #	Number Rolled	Count	Bet
1	4	1-count	0
2	11	2-count	0
3	5	3-count	0
4	6	4-count	0
5	*8	5-Count	$10 Come
6	9	Come bet goes to 9	Take Odds on the 9 $10 Come
7	8	Come bet goes to 8	Take Odds on 8 Put up new Come bet if you wish to be on three numbers

You can also go up on the Come before the 5-Count is completed, doing so after the 3-count or 4-count, but put Odds only after the 5-Count is completed. The longer you wait, the better for your bankroll. However, many players don't feel comfortable waiting for the full 5-Count if they are going the Come-betting route. Dom and I prefer to go up after the entire 5-Count is completed.

Example Five: Place Betting

Place betting with the 5-Count is very simple. When the 5-Count is completed, you Place the 6 and/or 8. If you wish to bet on the 4 and 10 or 5 and 9, make sure these are buyable, with the vig paid *only on wins*.

Shooter's Roll #	Number Rolled	Count	Bet
1	7	0-count	0
2	8	1-count	0
3	12	2-count	0
4	6	3-count	0
5	4	4-count	0
6	2	4-count/h	0
7	*9	5-Count	Place bet the 6 and 8; buy the 4 or 10 if vig is paid on winning bets only. Be up on no more than three numbers.

That Is Yours, This Is Mine

The 5-Count is the only shooter-selection system that has been proven to work in a massive study of 200 million simulated shooters. Check out the report on our website, www.goldentouchcraps.com. It makes you look like a regular player but keeps your risk quite low.

And there is also an added benefit, which we alluded to earlier. Sometimes the 5-Count can actually give you what we call a monetary edge over the casino—even against random rollers.

What About Going Up on the Darkside Right Away?

Some players, trying to outthink the brilliant Captain's 5-Count, think that going up on the Don't Pass or Don't Come before the 5-Count is finished is a way to play almost every roll with little risk. Not so. The very moment you put that Don't Pass or Don't Come bet, the casino's edge is 8-to-3 over you because the casino will win eight times on the 7 and 11 and the Don't bettor can win only three times on the 2 and 3. So you are just giving the casino more cracks at your bankroll going up before the 5-Count is finished. In fact, going up on the Don't Pass or Don't Come right away is the same as betting on all shooters and all rolls.

If you like to play the Darkside Don'ts, then wait until the 5-Count is finished, then bet a Don't Come (or Don't Pass) and when up on a number, take full Odds. The 5-Count works the same for Darkside random players as for Lightside random players. Every player should use it.

What the 5-Count Isn't

Some ploppies mistakenly think that the Captain used the appearance percentage of the 7 to the other numbers as the foundation of the 5-Count. He wasn't looking at averages or short-term results, not at all. He was looking at the totality of the game to save us money over extended periods of time. These ploppies then state: "How stupid the Captain is. With five rolls or more before you bet, the 7 is more likely to occur."

No it isn't.

The 7 has about a 17 percent chance of occurring in a random game at any time—now and forever. There is no more likelihood of the 7 appearing on the ninth roll than on the first roll than on the 50th roll. Players who think a number is more likely to appear because it hasn't appeared in a while are mistaken. In a random game, a number does not have more of a chance to come up than its probability indicates. It takes some time to see that this is so...*but it is so*. Ploppy critics try to outthink the Captain, which is a waste of their time...and ours.

The *Exact* Math

In the above discussion of the 5-Count, I did not use fractions. However, to be precise, Professor Stewart Ethier did a mathematical study of the 5-Count against *random rollers*, and here is what he found: the 5-Count players bet on 43.5 percent of the *random rolls* and did not bet on 56.5 percent of the random rolls. He took four rollers as examples so we could see what he means.

Roller No. 1: rolls 6, 8, 11, 9, 7-out (5 rolls: 5 no-bets)

Roller No. 2: rolls 4, 4, 7, 12, 3, 7, 9, **4, 6, 6, 8, 3, 11, 7-out** (14 rolls: 7 no-bets, 7 bets)

Roller No. 3: rolls 3, 7, 6, 10, 9, 6, 2, 8, **4, 9, 2, 5, 5, 8, 7, 6, 2, 5, 7-out** (19 rolls: 8 no-bets, 11 bets)

Roller No. 4: rolls 11, 9, 7-out (3 rolls: 3 no-bets)

Roller No. 1 survives five rolls but does not achieve the 5-Count. You do not bet on Roller No. 1. Roller No. 2 survives 14 rolls, achieving the 5-Count on the seventh roll. You bet only on his last seven rolls in bold. Roller No. 3 survives 19 rolls, achieving the 5-Count on the eighth roll. You bet only on his last 11 rolls in bold. Roller No. 4 survives three rolls but does not achieve 5-Count. You do not bet on Roller No. 4.

Professor Ethier summarized what his mathematical analysis found: "In the example, you eliminate two of four rollers, or 50 percent of the random rollers. Long-term percentage is 48.6 percent. In the example, you make no bet on 23 of 41 random rolls, or 56 percent. Long-term percentage is 56.5 percent. To state the converse: in the example, you bet on two of four rollers, or 50 percent. Long-term percentage is 51.4 percent. In the example, you bet on 18 of 41 rolls, or 44 percent. Long-term percentage is 43.5 percent."

Stewart Ethier is professor of mathematics at the University of Utah and has long had an interest in craps. For example, he wrote "Improving On Bold Play at Craps" in the journal *Operations Research*.

APPENDIX II

The Captain's Greatest Roll

July 2005: The Captain called me at 11:00 one night, which is late for him and late for me, and he wanted to know if I wanted to make a trip with him to Atlantic City very early the next morning. It would just be a single day, to play, to talk, to walk, to reminisce. Naturally I said, "Of course!" I never miss an opportunity to meet with the Captain, even if it means a day trip that takes three and a half hours. From Long Island to Atlantic City is a long haul.

I had just gotten back from a graduation party for my niece, Melanie, and I was tired. I had not practiced my dice throw since May when we did *The Frank Scoblete Gamblers Jamboree* in Canada. I'd been working on a new book, and I had not planned to play craps until I got to Vegas in mid-September so, sad but true, I got lazy. I decided that a late night's practice would probably not help me much since I had to get up at 4:00 the next morning. Better to go to sleep and dream about not embarrassing myself the next day in Atlantic City.

By now just about all savvy craps players know who the Captain is. Aside from being the greatest craps player of all time, the Captain is my mentor, the man who taught me more about proper gambling in practice and in theory than I have learned from all the books and articles I have ever read.

I have met most of the greats of casino gambling, but the Captain stands alone. I am reminded of Hemingway's *The Old Man and the Sea*, when Manolin is expressing fear about the Yankees not being able to win the pennant. Santiago states, "There are many good ballplayers and some great ones, but there is only DiMaggio." DiMaggio wasn't just a great ballplayer; he was *the* ballplayer.

There is only the Captain.

The Captain is the true master of the game of craps. Long before I wrote my first words about how to beat the modern casino craps game with dice control in the late 1980s, the Captain and the Arm were beating Atlantic City casinos steadily from the late 1970s and through the 1980s and into the mid-1990s when the Arm had to retire due to severe arthritis.

I was happy that the Captain shared his secrets with me, that he allowed me to write about how to succeed at craps, and I was privileged to see him and the Arm shoot countless times over those years. The Captain is a great shooter, but the Arm was the greatest I ever saw, and I have seen the great ones, many of whom are my colleagues in GTC.

The Captain, now past his mid-eighties and hopefully heading for 90, has lost just about all of his high-rolling friends, known as "the Crew." Jimmy P., Little Vic, Russ the Breather, Frank the fearful, the Doctor, and the Judge are all now playing craps in the heavenly kingdom where dice control isn't necessary because all rolls are perfect but still thrilling.

One remaining Crew member of the Captain's, now known as Satch (Dave), is an instructor in the GTC dice-control seminars. He was the youngest of the Captain's crew.

Thankfully, I did not have to drive down to Atlantic City. The Captain had the limo pick me up at 4:30 AM, and then we picked him up in New York City. Usually the Captain drives down to AC with his wife, or he takes the high-roller bus where all the "old guys" (as he calls them) play poker on their way to the shore. What I find fascinating about him is the fact that despite his staggering wins at the game and his success in his businesses, the Captain doesn't have that high roller "give me, give me" attitude. He is a humble man. Greatness and humility are a rare combination in the gambling world, where the biggest morons often have the most bloated egos.

In the limo on the way to Atlantic City, the Captain said, "I'm sad, Frank. The Arm is very sick, and it doesn't look as if she is going to improve. Her husband thinks she is preparing to go." [The Arm passed away on June 6, 2007.]

The Arm was also in her mid-eighties, and the years had not been kind to her. I saw her about a year prior, and she was shrunken, bent, and a little distant, as if she were having a hard time holding herself together. The Captain could walk eight miles up and down the Boardwalk in Atlantic City, but the Arm could barely walk across a room. I don't know if it was my father or the Captain who first said to me, "Getting old is a slow process, but one day you fall off a cliff." The Arm seemed to have fallen off the cliff.

"What does she have?" I asked him.

"Age," he said.

The Captain had a wistful look. I changed the subject.

"You've been keeping track of your rolls?" I asked.

"Most times, now, I use chips like you said. In the old days," smiled the Captain, "the fun of going to Atlantic City was that I played with a whole bunch of friends and I also was able to win money. I had friendship and a challenge all wrapped together. It went very fast. The time. It flew."

It does fly. I am at the stage in my own life where I see that time has flown. My sons—my *little* boys, whose small hands I could consume in mine—are now men. I see pictures of them when they were little, and I can still feel the *feel* of them from those times. I can almost go back in time, almost but not quite. I am a grandfather, too: John Charles and Danielle.

Time.

"You know," said the Captain. "I live more in the past now than in the present. I watch the old movies. Cary Grant, Ingrid Bergman, Ronald Colman. I don't even know today's stars. My generation merely lingers now. We fought Hitler, the Japanese, and Mussolini. We defeated the great enemies of mankind, and now we just linger."

In Atlantic City, the time was only 8:30 AM when we checked in, but the casino had a suite ready for us. One of the Captain's good friends is a high ranker at one of the biggest casinos, and he made sure that the two-story suite was ready for the Captain's day at the Queen of Resorts.

"Let's put our stuff in the room," said the Captain. Room? It was six rooms! But to the Captain it was a room.

"Then let's take a little walk," said the Captain.

"Fine," I said.

We put our bags in the suite. The Captain took one of the bedrooms; I took the other. Mine was actually the better bedroom because I had my own Jacuzzi in it.

We took a walk along the Boardwalk. The Captain and his departed Crew once owned this town. They were $1,000-plus bettors. And that was way back when.

"Atlantic City is actually nicer now than it was in 1978, when it was really a ghetto," said the Captain. "The buildings in those days were falling down all over town. It isn't Vegas, but Vegas isn't Vegas anymore either."

We walked for about an hour and a half, and the Captain recommended that we go back to the room, rest a little, and then hit the tables. The Captain is a firm believer that you have to play rested and that you must never allow the casino's 24-hour-a-day rhythm to overwhelm you. I learned that lesson the hard way when my wife and I lost all our gambling money on one trip because I had played stupidly—overbetting my bankroll and going on tilt. The Captain taught me then how to keep my normal human rhythm in the face of the 24-hour bam, bam, bam of the casino.

In the suite, the Captain went to his room. I lay down on the bed in my room. The Captain did seem wistful, and his perkiness was not at the usual level. *The Arm's deterioration must be weighing heavily on him*, I thought. He and the Arm had won millions together. They had been on the crest of the first wave of the dice-control revolution.

It's funny, but I never think of people dying. I never think of myself as dying.

I counted up the people I have been close to who have died. I reached only 20, and that includes my grandparents.

The Captain went to a high school class reunion a few years prior, and there were only five of his classmates left alive.

Now we just linger.

The Captain was a part of the greatest generation. He had been in the army air corps in World War II. He had been shot down behind enemy lines in the Philippines and had to survive for more than a week hiding from the Japanese soldiers who scoured the jungle looking for Americans who had been shot down. He caught malaria, to boot. He saw the Enola Gay land at his army air base. He served in Japan during the occupation. He's a fascinating guy. I think of him as a hero.

Now we just linger.

An hour or so later, we were heading for the casino floor. The Captain said he had actually fallen asleep. I must have too since the time went by in the blink of an eye.

Time.

The casino was crowded, but we found our two spots open at a 12-foot table. I was on stick left one and the Captain was on stick right one. I also noticed that the Captain had gotten shorter in the past few years. He used to be my height, but he had gotten an inch or two shorter. He was in good shape, but time had also diminished him somewhat.

The pit boss came over and said hello to him. The Captain took out a marker. The Captain's betting had decreased somewhat from his glory days of the 1980s. I took a marker as well.

In Atlantic City, it usually takes a while for the marker to arrive. Unlike Vegas, you don't get your chips until you actually sign the marker. So we had to wait. While we were waiting two hosts came over to say hello to the Captain. They knew him as "the Captain" too. What interests me all the more is why the people who know who the Captain is don't tell others. These two hosts, longtime Atlantic City people, knew him. Three of the casinos' biggest honchos in Atlantic City know who he is, too. Indeed, he has some good friends in Atlantic City who work for the casinos. They were kids when he started his craps career, some of them craps dealers, and now they run places. And they still come to him for advice.

Time.

We waited for our markers as the hosts departed.

No big deal. The dice were two people to my left with a squirrelly fellow. He established the 5 as his point, rolled a couple of times, and sevened out. I wanted the markers to come to us just as the Captain was about to roll. Then we wouldn't be wasting any money on random rollers.

When the shooter just before the Captain got the dice, our markers came. "Sorry this took so long," said the floor woman. "We're a little understaffed today."

The Captain signed for his marker and I signed for mine.

We were playing at a 5X Odds table with a $10 minimum bet. Both of us 5-Counted the shooter next to the Captain. He made it to the 4-count and sevened out.

It became the Captain's turn. I placed a $15 Pass Line bet, and the Captain placed a $30 Pass Line bet. The Captain rolled a 6 as his point. The Captain sets the 3V set at all times, even though he keeps his bets off during the come-out roll, which is perhaps not the optimal way to play when setting dice that way. However, the Captain thinks of the come-out roll as a rest period when he shoots.

I studied him a few times during his rolls that day, and indeed on the come-out roll, his intensity was not as great. He was *resting*.

He put up a $300 bet on the 8 and he bought the 4 for $55, paying a $2 vig. He put $250 in Odds behind his Pass Line bet of 6. This betting was more than I had seen him bet in the past few years, and I wondered why he had upped his action. I had $125 in Odds behind the point, and I had $150 on the 8. I also bought the 4 for $55, as I would mirror the Captain's betting. If you are going to imitate, you might as well imitate the best.

By betting $15 or $30 on the Pass/Come at a 5X Odds game, the casino we were playing in allowed you to "push the house" up on the odds. So you could take $75 for $15 on the Pass/Come or $150 for $30 on the Pass/Come on the 4 and 10, $100 or $200 on the 5 and 9, and $125 or $250 on the 6 and 8. The Captain is a master at "pushing the house," as he was the first player to get Atlantic City casinos to allow you to buy the 4 or 10 for $35 paying just a $1 vig. He even pushed some casinos to allow you to buy the 4 or 10 for $39 for the same $1 vig.

The Captain rolled a 5, a 10, and then he sevened out.

It was my turn.

"Hey, hey, Frank?" said a voice next to me.

"Yes?" I said.

"Kenneth Frasca," he said. "I went to your Jamboree two years ago."

"Hi," I said.

"Put your Pass Line bet up, sir," said the stickman, tapping the Pass Line with the stick.

I placed my $15 on the Pass Line.

"You going to get in?" I asked.

"He's coming to lunch with me," said the woman next to him.

"My wife. Linda, this is Frank Scoblete, the writer, you met him at the Jamboree," he said.

"Hi, Linda," I said and shook her hand.

"Sir, we're waiting for you," said the stickman.

"Okay," I said. "Sorry."

"Hey, the Captain ain't around is he?" joked Kenneth.

"He's on stick right," I said as I took the dice.

"Let's go to lunch," said his wife.

"Oh, Jesus, oh, Jesus, Linda that's the Captain!"

"I'm starving," said Linda.

Kenneth went over and said hello to the Captain. I forgot about Kenneth and rolled

I took the dice and set for the 7. I hit 11, then two 7s in a row, then a 5. That was my point. I took $100 in Odds on my point of 5. I placed $150 on the 6 and $150 on the 8. I also used the 3V set. I rolled a 6 and was paid $175 for it. I rolled another 6. Then I rolled a third 6. Then I sevened out.

My dice were looking good, and I figured I would have a good roll next turn. Little did I know there would be no next turn.

We 5-Counted all the shooters. Four of the eight at the table made it through the 5-Count and we put up $10 Come bets on them with double Odds. We lost money on them as they all sevened out soon after we had some bets up.

A lot of players don't realize that the 5-Count really does not reduce the house edge on random rollers. It just reduces by 57 percent what you bet on random rollers, thus saving you money. However, as Dr. Don Catlin showed in a massive study of 200 million simulated shooters, if you are at a table with controlled shooters, even if you don't know they are controlled shooters, the 5-Count gets you on them 11 percent more often than a normal player will be. That's where you can make some money.

We GTC dice controllers use the 5-Count to reduce the number of rolls we bet on, and on random rollers we also bet much lower than we will on controlled shooters. The 5-Count is a wonderful tool in a controlled shooter's arsenal if he has to play at the same table as random rollers, which most of us do. As you can see, my total risk on the random rollers who made it through the 5-Count that day was a mere $30. Odds don't count since they are a break-even bet with the house.

The Captain got the dice again. The Captain is a calm shooter, second in calmness to the Arm herself. Nothing gets to him. I have rarely seen him lose his temper at the tables. He doesn't practice Zen, but he is very Zenlike.

The Captain set the 3V and rolled. It was 1:15 in the afternoon. He hit a 2. Then he hit a 3. Then he established his point, a 4. We were going up the number scale! The Captain put up $300 on the 6 and 8 and $150 in Odds behind his point. I had $150 placed on my 6 and 8 and $75 behind my Pass Line bet.

The Captain rolled a few numbers we weren't on and then hit a 6. Then he hit the 8. Then the 6 again. Then he made the 4. The table gave polite applause. The Captain now added a $55 buy of the 10 to his bets. I did the same.

In Atlantic City, if you want to buy the 4 or 10 for $55, you pay a $2 vig, but if you put up both numbers at the same time, you must pay $5 total. So, the way to bet to save that $1 is to make a bet of one number, then after a roll, bet the other number. Those dollars add up. Unfortunately in Atlantic City, you must pay the vig up front on buy bets, which means you pay that vig on winning and losing rolls. In many casinos around the country, the vig is only extracted on the buy bets after you win but not on any losses. That cuts the house edge down considerably.

The Captain established his point, a 6. We both bought the 4 for $55. We took our 6 Place bets down and took Odds behind the Pass Line point of 6.

So we were up on four numbers, the 4, 6, 8, and 10. And the Captain rolled. He became very focused because he could seven out. And he started hitting numbers. At a certain point he made his point of 6. He then made several more points and many numbers.

The Captain was hot. Other players joined the table.

At the 25-minute mark, the Captain had rolled 32 numbers—one green chip, one red chip, and two white chips—and the Captain was on another come-out roll. Then he did something that was unusual for him.

"Frank," he said. "Can you get me a chair?"

Since the mid-1980s when I first started to play craps with the Captain, I don't think I ever saw him sit down. I was startled. But I quickly went over to an empty blackjack table and grabbed a chair. I set it behind the Captain. He sat on it right away.

The floor woman came over and said, "I'm sorry, you can't sit there." Just as quickly, the pit boss came over and touched the floor woman on the arm and said, "He's the exception. Let him sit if he wants to." The floor woman looked confused but obeyed her boss. The two of them walked away, and when they were on the other end of the pit, they started to talk. I have no idea what they were saying, but they both kept shooting glances our way.

On the come-out roll, all our bets, except our Pass Line bets obviously, were off. The Captain gently lofted the dice down the table. He rolled a 7 and then established a point of 6.

From there on in, it started to get blurry. The Captain rolled numbers and points. I was counting the rolls, putting white chips down, then reds, and then a second green. We were at 45 minutes and the Captain had rolled 54 numbers. On his come-out rolls and when the dealers were paying off the bets, he would sit in the chair and just stare straight ahead. He was locked into some kind of meditative state. I never said a word to him. I had bets on all the numbers and had pressed them once, twice, or three times depending on how often they had hit.

The third green chip went down. The Captain was at 75 numbers. I looked over at him. He did not look at all tired, just reflective, sedate, as if he were in another world. In January 2004, the Captain had rolled 100 numbers—an amazing roll. I wondered if he could reach that plateau again. One hundred numbers is a magic roll.

76 numbers.

The Captain has a very easy throw. There is no strain in him when he shoots. He is focused. He is in total control of himself.

77 numbers.

He is in total control of the dice. His roll is the model for the Golden Touch roll.

78 numbers.

The Captain made a point. I had three green chips and three white chips for the 78 numbers. The cocktail waitress came over, and the Captain ordered an orange juice, no ice, and I ordered bottled water.

"When you come over with the drinks," I said to the waitress, "bring me his drink if he's still rolling, okay?" I put $5 on her tray.

"Okay," she said.

Kenneth Frasca reappeared. I squeezed over so he could get next to me. The table was now packed.

"How's he doing? How did he do last roll?" asked Frasca.

"It's the same roll. He's at 78 numbers," I said.

"Oh, man!" he whispered in my ear.

"I thought we were going to walk the Boardwalk?" asked Linda.

"Not now," said Kenneth, who bought in. Linda did not seem pleased. But she wandered away. The Captain had no magic for her.

As the Captain shot his come-out roll, new chips were brought in. We had seriously damaged the casino's chip area, and new chips, big and little denominations both, were now being counted on the table.

The Captain ignored it. He rolled. He established a point.

79 numbers.

Most of the other players were now betting green and black chips. Somewhere around roll 45, most of the players started to press their bets. Some had become almost insanely aggressive. The table was full of players now—13 players altogether, seven on my side with Frasca squeezed in, and six on the Captain's side.

80 numbers (three green chips, one red).

81 numbers (three green chips, one red, one white).

There were only a few hardway bets, an unusual situation during a big roll. It was almost as if no one wanted to slow down the game with bets that take too long to pay off. Most of the players were good bettors—a rarity at a craps table but one that was making this game progress at a nice pace.

The Captain was in his rolling zone for sure.

82 numbers.

83 numbers.

84 numbers.

85 numbers (three greens, two reds).

The Captain is a rarity. I am not. As a writer, a teacher, and a speaker, as a former actor, I crave the public performance. I want a readership, an audience. I like the spotlight on me.

86 numbers.

The Captain doesn't care about those things. He was the leader of "the Crew" because they made him the leader. He didn't ask for it. His nature must make other men and women want to follow him.

87 numbers.

He never asked to share in the glory or profits of the books or tapes I wrote. He never asked to be on television or radio. He never asked me to write about him. He did his thing, and he let the world do its thing.

88 numbers.

Best-selling gaming author Henry Tamburin asked me, "How come the Captain doesn't want to go out in public and be recognized?" I told Henry the Captain is the guy everyone wants us to be. "You see when we are criticized, some of it is, 'Well, if they are so good, why are they writing about it? Why aren't they just doing it?' Well, the Captain is the guy who did it and is still doing it. He doesn't crave the public attention like we do."

89 numbers.

I had hit 89 numbers. I wasn't keeping track of them, but Dominator and one of our Golden Touch students were. I had two students at the table that day.

90 numbers.

So much for 89! The Captain was getting close to the magic 100 rolls.

91 numbers.

The Captain was happy that I became successful as an advantage player and as a writer. He was happy my books sold so well. But he is content to do what he does.

92 numbers.

He has slowed down now. His investing in real estate is over. He lives off his past investments and his once-a-week play in Atlantic City.

93 numbers.

The Captain used to play several times a week. I can recall him in those days. He was probably 63 when I first played craps with him at the tables. He was not much older then than I am now. I first played craps at the Claridge, which was a great casino for players.

94 numbers.

"Pay the line!" shouted the stickman.

It was now another come-out roll. I remember this clearly. I put several stacks of black chips on the table to color them up. I was completely out of room in the chip rack in front of me. The Captain now sat for all the come-out rolls. Kenneth Frasca kept whispering in my ear, "I can't believe I'm playing with the Captain."

"Believe it," I said.

95 numbers (no point established—he rolled an 11).

96 numbers (another 11).

I noticed that the Captain's bets were with purple and orange chips now.

97 numbers (Point of 4 established).

We were getting close to 100 numbers. Would he make it?

98 numbers.

99 numbers.

I looked over at the Captain. He had no idea how many numbers he rolled, but the time was now 2:45 in the afternoon. He had rolled for one and a half hours.

He set the dice carefully. He aimed. I noticed that there were now several suits behind the boxman. Big money was being wagered at this table, and it was the job of the suits to make sure that no mistakes were made with such big money in play. I could see another cart loaded with chips being wheeled to the table. Some players think that the suits gather on a hot game to cool it off. That is not so. They gather to make sure the money is being handled properly. With $500 and $1,000 chips in play, a small mistake can cost a lot of money—to the casino and to the players too.

"This is number 100?" asked Frasca.

"Yes," I whispered.

"Oh, man," he whispered.

The Captain arced the dice, giving them a gentle backspin. They hit the table, moved slowly to the back wall, and died flat, dead at the base of the pyramids, having barely glanced off the back wall.

"Five! Five!" shouted the stickman. "No field five!"

That was 100 rolls. That was one black chip. That was, my God, 100 numbers for the Captain!

No one other than Frasca and I knew what a monumental moment this was, but they all knew they were on one hell of a roll.

101 numbers.

102 numbers.

103 numbers.

The new chips were brought in. One of the suits laughingly said, "This is it, guys, these are our last chips. Don't take them all from us."

104 numbers.

105 numbers.

106 numbers.

Then a bloated man at the end of the table started an argument. "I had a $5 yo bet! Where's my money?"

"That was the roll before this one, sir, not this one. It's a one-roll bet, sir," said the dealer.

"Call over the floor man," said the bloated one.

I took $80 in chips and threw them over to the man.

"Forget the floor man," I said.

"I, uh, I..." said the large one.

"Take the chips and let this man roll for God's sake!" I said. The dope took the chips.

"Move the dice," said the boxman. "We don't want this table to cool down."

The stickman pushed the dice over to the Captain. He had been seated while the bloated one had stupidly slowed down the game. The Captain now stood, set the dice, aimed, and released.

107 numbers.

That was nice of the boxman to say he wanted the hot roll to continue. He would not be able to share in the massive amount of tips the Captain, several players, and I were giving the dealers on each and every roll, but he looked genuinely happy that he was watching such a great afternoon's session.

108 numbers.

Several players and the Captain had now reached table-maximum bets on some of the numbers.

109 numbers.

110 numbers.

111 numbers.

Which got me to thinking, *Stanley Fujitake! The record.*

112 numbers.

Fujitake held the dice for three hours and six minutes. He did this on May 18, 1989, at the California Club in downtown Las Vegas. That feat earned him the title of "the Golden Arm." A whole inventory of spectacular tales has grown up around the man who held the record for the longest craps hand in history.

113 numbers.

Sure, others claimed anonymously that they saw shooters surpass that record, but only Stanley Fujitake's record was taken seriously by anyone the least interested in craps. He did his feat in front of scores of witnesses, and the time was verified by them and by the casino.

114 numbers.

Fujitake's was *the* record.

115 numbers.

How incredible was *the* record? Take Joe DiMaggio's 56-game hitting streak, Wilt Chamberlain's 100 points in an NBA game, Muhammad Ali's upset of George Foreman, Secretariat's winning of the Triple Crown in stunning blowouts, and wrap them all up in a knot—Fujitake's record is more spectacular.

116 numbers.

Three hours and six minutes! That might have been 200 rolls of the dice.

117 numbers.

Fujitake. *The record.*

118 numbers.

I looked over at the Captain just as he looked at me. A smile played on his lips. "I feel good," he said to me.

119 numbers.

Of course, Fujitake was a random roller and not a controlled shooter as is the Captain. His great feat is the great feat of luck, while the Captain's great feats—and he has had many great feats—are the results of skill. While the Captain was rolling, I had no idea that he had actually beaten the number of rolls Fujitake had in 1989—which was 118 rolls before he sevened out.

120 numbers.

The stickmen at this casino were courteous, as they moved back as the Captain threw. That gave him a clear vision down the table. The player at the end of the table never put his Pass Line bet down where the Captain landed his dice. That was very smart of him. The table was behaving as you would want the table to behave to help create and perpetuate the monster roll.

121 numbers.

There were maybe 30 people standing around the outside of the table watching. Frasca kept whispering, "Holy shit" in my ear. That was his day's religious mantra. An aggressive-looking guy with slicked-back black hair was about to try to squeeze in next to the Captain as the Captain was lifting the dice. The guy next to the Captain pushed the aggressive one and said, "Don't even think about it." The guy next to the Captain sounded and looked like a wiseguy and the aggressive guy slunk away, his girlfriend hanging on his arm saying, "Why can't we get in and play? Why can't we get in and play?"

122 numbers.

123 numbers.

124 numbers.

For almost 20 years the Captain and his Crew owned Atlantic City. High rollers, fun lovers, 22 of the most interesting men and women one could ever meet. Strangely only one of them ever really understood that the Captain was winning all those years. His name was Jimmy P. In the early 1990s, Jimmy P., the Captain, and the Arm hit Tropworld (now Tropicana) for millions in wins and comps.

125 numbers (one black chip and one green chip).

126 numbers.

This roll was the longest roll I had ever seen. Even the Arm never had a roll that was this long. At 126 numbers, the Captain was approaching two hours of rolling. I remember one of the executives, who worked at the Claridge, saying in 1992, "The Captain is killing us." Even the former president of the Claridge wrote about the Captain and his Crew in a book. He talked about how the Captain hammered them.

Yet no one has revealed the Captain's name. Interesting.

127 numbers.

The length of a hand kept in time is not as descriptive as the length of a hand kept in number of rolls.

128 numbers.

129 numbers.

This roll was in the mega numbers.

130 numbers (one black, one green, one red).

We were at the two-hour mark now. Two hours of rolling the dice. The Captain would roll, sit in the chair as the payouts were made, then stand when the stickman moved the dice to him. He constantly set the 3V. He was a machine. No, in fact, more accurately, he was in a gambling ballet. His every move was smooth and beautiful.

131 numbers (one black, one green, one red, one white).

How much luck did the Captain need to create this monster-of-monsters hand? He had rolled some 7s on the come out. The 3V is not a set for rolling 7s, and those 7s were therefore mistakes. That was good luck for him and for the rest of us at the table. He rolled at least four 7s that I remember on the come out. Had any one of those 7s been during the point cycle of the game, he would have sevened out.

132 numbers.

133 numbers.

Good luck? I have had great good luck in my life. I have wonderful parents, a wonderful wife, wonderful children, wonderful grandchildren, a wonderful writing career, and I have a few good friends too.

134 numbers.

135 numbers.

I also have some people who—for God knows what reason!—hate me and hate my writing. Walter Thomason, the gambling writer, used to tease me by sending me Internet web posts by people who were attacking me. One famous though highly pompous gambling authority whose books are poor sellers once said he would kill himself if he woke up and found out he had turned into me. As Golden Touch has become internationally known, the attacks have become even fiercer. As the beautiful AP says, "No one kicks a dead dog."

136 numbers.

137 numbers.

138 numbers.

The Captain and the Arm were the most devastating one-two punch in the history of modern casino craps. The two of them won eight figures together. Although Atlantic City is not allowed to bar players, Tropworld refused to give them any comps after they won $1.5 million in a few months. Trop even sent a letter around telling the other casinos to be aware of these two. I was able to read this letter when the Captain showed it to me. He got it from one of his casino-executive friends.

139 numbers.

The Captain was in a rhythm.

140 numbers.

Bing!

141 numbers.

Bing!

142 numbers.

Bing!

143 numbers.

Bing!

144 numbers.

Bing!

We were at 144 numbers! *There is only the Captain.* The very Captain who was now banging away at two hours and 15 minutes in a roll that would become legendary.

145 numbers.

Bing!

146 numbers.

Bing!

I looked over at the Captain, who was as calm as he was when he first got the dice. *There is only the Captain. There is only the Captain. There is only the Captain.* Could he go to 200 numbers? Could he go for over three hours and six minutes?

147 numbers.

Bing!

The Captain is the greatest craps player who ever lived. He is more than a master, more than a mentor. *There is only the Captain.* He was at two hours and 18 minutes and had hit 147 numbers.

Now we just linger. Time. There is only the Captain.

He lofted into the air. One die lagged a little, and when they came down that lagging die just stopped dead. The other die went to the back wall, hit, and gently rolled over.

There was a pause. Time stopped.

"Call it," said the boxman.

"Seven," said the stickman, "Seven out! Line away, pay the Don'ts."

There were no Don'ts. There was only silence.

Now we just linger.

Time.

There is only the Captain.

"That was a great roll," I said.

"Oh, God," said Frasca.

"Great roll, sir," said the boxman.

"Great roll, Captain," said the Pit Boss.

"Great roll, Captain," said one of the other suits.

And then the applause started. The players and the spectators started to clap. It became thunderous. Even the boxman clapped. The stickman, with the stick under his arm, clapped too. Then people cheered and some yelled, "Bravo! Bravo!"

That roll lasted two hours 18 minutes. It was 147 numbers, with the 148th number being the seven out.

The guy next to Frasca said to us, "They called him the Captain? Is that *the* Captain? *The* Captain?"

"Yes," said Frasca as if he knew the Captain a long, long time.

"You know him?" asked the man.

"Yes," I said. "We know him." I included Frasca in the "we." Frasca smiled.

"My God, I can't believe it," said the man. "I saw the Captain himself. Oh, my God," he said as he put down his stacks of black, purple, and orange chips.

"Yes, you did," I said. "That is the man himself."

"Amazing," said Frasca. "One hundred forty-seven numbers."

"One hundred forty-seven numbers," said the man. "God."

No one can take this achievement away from the Captain—147 numbers, two hours 18 minutes of rolling. The man who first realized that rhythmic rolling, a synonym for dice control, was the way to beat the house in 1978, the man who figured out how to win money playing craps, had just completed a Babe Ruthian roll. Ruth once hit a baseball 626 feet, the longest home run in history. And this was the longest craps roll in history—147 numbers.

There is only the Captain.

We colored up our mound of chips, and security escorted us to the cage.

"We'll have a late lunch in the suite, and then we'll head back home," said the Captain.

"You rolled 147 numbers, Captain," I said.

"It was a great roll," he said.

Yes, it was.

There is only the Captain.

[On May 23, 2009, random roller Patricia DeMauro rolled 154 numbers, breaking the Captain's world record. Her achievement is completely chronicled in my book *Casino Craps: Shoot to Win!*]

APPENDIX III
Dice Positions
and Dice Sets

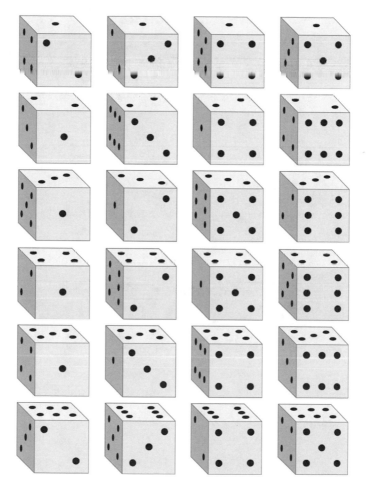

Dice Sets

Here is a list of various dice sets that you can use in traditional and radical betting approaches:

Hardway Sets:

T5F4:T5F4

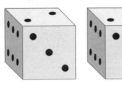

T4F2:T4F2

T2F3:T2F3

T3F5:T3F5

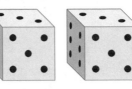

T5F3:T5F3

T3F2:T3F2

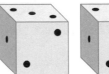

T2F4:T2F4

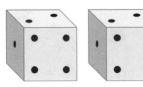

T4F5:T4F5

3V Sets:

T3F5:T3F1

T2F3:T6F3

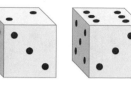

T4F2:T4F6

T5F4:T1F4

T3F6:T3F2

T1F3:T5F3

T4F1:T4F5

T6F4:T2F4

Hop 2:4 Set:

T2F4:T4F2

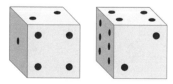

Hop 1:5 Set:
T1F5:T5F1

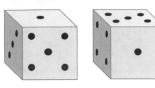

All-7s Sets:

T2F4:T5F3   **T3F2:T4F5**

T5F3:T2F4   **T4F5:T3F2**

      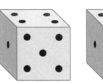

T5F4:T2F3   **T3F5:T4F2**

T2F3:T5F4   **T4F2:T3F5**

Whirl, Horn, Buy 3, Buy 11 Set:
T1F5:T2F6

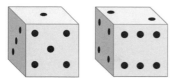

Buy 2, Buy 12 Set:
T1F5:T1F5

Glossary

401G Account: A bank account or money-market fund where a player keeps his gambling bankroll. The *G* stands for gambling.

5-Count: The Captain's method for eliminating 57 percent of the random rolls. Players who use the 5-Count will only bet on 43 percent of random rolls. In terms of comping, most 5-Counters have found they get the same comps for less risk because their body time is counted, not their risk time.

Action: The amount of money being bet at a table or the amount of money an individual bets.

Ada from Decatur: The 8.

Advantage Play: Casino play where the player has the edge over the casino as he does when utilizing dice control.

Any Craps: A one-roll bet on the numbers 2, 3, and 12.

Any Seven: A one-roll bet on the 7. Also known as Big Red.

Arm, the: The woman considered by Frank and the Captain to be the greatest dice controller of all time.

Axis: Think of the dice glued next to each other with a stick going through the middle of both of them. The stick represents the axis around which the dice spin. Whenever we set the dice, there is an invisible axis going through the middle of them.

Axis Control: The ability to keep the dice on axis more than probability indicates.

Backline: Old term for Don't Pass.

Back Wall: Sides of the table covered with foam-rubber pyramids that should be hit with each shot. These are there to randomize dice rolls.

Backward Testing: How the dice finish their landing after hitting the back wall determines whether your throw needs help or is fine. If the dice look fine, then no change is needed in a player's setup and throw.

Bar: Refers to a tie bet on the come-out roll for Darkside players. The 12 will not win or lose for the Don't player. Some casinos will bar the 2 instead of the 12. Also sometimes refers to players who have been told they can't play a certain game or in a certain casino.

Barber Poll: Bets made with various colored chips, often not arranged in denomination order, high on bottom, low on top.

Below Random: The mistaken idea that something can be less than random. A dice throw is either random or controlled. There is no such thing as less than random or more than random. We sometimes use the phrase "worse than random" in this book as slang, but it is not to be taken literally.

Bet-All Players: Players who bet on every roll of the dice or on all shooters from the beginning of their rolls.

Beveled Dice: Fixed dice.

Biased Dice: Dice that are fixed to favor certain dice faces over others. Also called Fixed Dice.

Big 6: Even-money bet in the bottom corners of some craps tables.

Big 8: Even-money bet in the bottom corners of some craps tables.

Big Dick: The number 10.

Big Red: A one-roll bet on the 7. Also known as Any Seven.

Blacks: Chips usually worth $100.

Blues: Chips usually worth $1.

Body Time: How long a player stays at a table. Bets are not necessarily or always at risk during the player's body time at the table.

Bones: Another name for dice. Original dice were probably made from the bones of animals and perhaps people.

Bouncy Tables: Tables where the surface causes the dice to bounce more than they would on a traditional table. There are various kinds of bounciness, and each has to be handled in different ways by the dice controller.

Bowl: Where the dice are kept in front of the stickman.

Boxcars: A 6:6 combination of the dice equaling the number 12.

Box Numbers: The 4, 5, 6, 8, 9, and 10 that appear in boxes at the top of the layout. Also known as Point Numbers.

Box Person: Individual who sits between the dealers. He is responsible for cashing in players' money, counting out chips, and making sure payouts are correct. He also settles most of the disputes at the table.

Boys, the: Synonym for dealers.

Browns: Chips usually worth $5,000.

Buffalo: A bet on all the hardways and on the Any Seven.

Buy Bet: Paying a commission to get true odds, as opposed to house odds, on certain Place bets.

Buying a Player's Don't Bet: Paying a small fee to take over a Don't bet when the Darkside player wishes to take that bet down. This can give the "buyer" an edge over the game.

Call Bet: Making a bet without any money or chips showing in one's hand. Usually not accepted.

Capped Dice: Biased or fixed dice.

Captain, the: The world's greatest craps player and thinker. He is the developer of the 5-Count and of controlled shooting, also known as Rhythmic Rolling and Dice Influence.

Card Counting: Keeping track of the relationship of high cards to low cards. Speed Count is an example of card counting that is extremely easy to learn.

Casino Cage or Cage: The "bank" of the casino where players can cash in their chips, receive markers for slot play, and cash in some coupons or checks.

Charting and Charting Tables: Checking to see what trends were happening at a given table or with a given shooter. If the game is random, all charting is a waste of time.

Checks: Another name for chips.

Chicken Feeders: Another name for Random Rollers, because some shooters throw the dice in a way that looks as if they are feeding chickens.

Chips: Tokens used as money at casino table games.

Chip Tray: Holds chips. Often called Rail in craps.

Cocked Dice: Dice that land against a chip or against the wall in a slanted manner. The stickman will make the call based on what number would come up if the chip had continued the way it was going.

Color Up or Color: Player hands in chips at the table when finished with play to get higher-denomination chips.

Come Bet: After a shooter's point is established, a bet that can be made during the point cycle of the game. The first placement of bet will win on the 7 or 11 and lose on the 2, 3, or 12. Once up on a box number, the bet wins if the number is hit and loses if a 7 is thrown.

Come-Out Roll: The shooter's first roll(s) before establishing a point. Wins on the 7 or 11 and loses on the 2, 3, or 12. If a shooter makes his point, the come-out roll occurs again. If a shooter sevens out, shooter gives dice up and next shooter gets them.

Comps or Complimentary: Casino gifts to the players such as food, drink, free or discounted hotel rooms, parties, presents, sporting or special events, etc. Comps are based on the casino's analysis of what types of losses the player is expected to have. These are known as Theoretical Losses.

Contract Bets: Pass Line point number and Come bets that cannot be taken down or called off once on a number. These are two-part bets where part one (come-out or first-come placement) favors the players and part two (the point or box number) favors the casinos. For the casinos to make money they must be able to have part two favor them in order to overcome players' edge in part one.

Controlled Shooters: Someone who can change the probabilities of the game by his throw of the dice. Also known as Rhythmic Rolling and Dice Influencing, among other terms.

Correspondence: The tendency for dice to make many rolls that mimic single and double pitches.

Crapless Craps: The 2, 3, 11, and 12 can be points. There are no Don't bets.

Crapping Out: Rolling a 2, 3, or 12 on the come-out roll. It is *not* a term for sevening out.

Craps Numbers: The 2, 3, and 12.

Crazy-Ball Tables: Table surfaces that cause the dice to behave as if they are crazy balls, bouncing this way and that. These are the most bouncy tables to be found in the casinos.

Crazy Crapper Bets: High-house-edge bets. Most of these are in the center of the layout.

Crossroader: A cheat or thief.

Darkside or Darksider: The Don't bets. A Darksider is a person who makes Don't bets.

Dead Table: A table where no one is playing or a table where shooters have had a series of early seven outs.

Dependent Trial Game: A game where what happened before has an impact on what happens next. An example is blackjack. If all aces have come out, no one can get a blackjack.

Devil, the: A term for the 7.

Dice Influencing: Someone who can change the probabilities of the game by his throw of the dice. Also known as Rhythmic Rolling and Controlled Shooting, among other terms.

Dice Set: A specific arrangement of dice before a shooter throws them.

Do Players: Betting with the number (or point) and against the 7. A player who bets the Pass Line, Come bet, Place bets, and Crazy Crapper bets where he is rooting for the number to appear. Also known as Lightside or Rightside and as Right betting.

Doey-Don't: Betting both the Pass Line and Don't Pass simultaneously. Betting both the Come and Don't Come simultaneously.

Don't Come: Bet placed after shooter's point is established. First placement wins on the 2 or 3, loses on the 7 or 11, and pushes on the 12 (sometimes the 2 and 12 are substituted for each other). Once up on a number, bet wins if shooter rolls a 7 and the bet loses if the shooter rolls the number.

Don't Pass: Opposite of the Pass Line. On the come-out roll, player wins if a 2 or 3 is rolled; he loses if a 7 or 11 is rolled; he ties if a 12 is rolled (sometimes the 2 and 12 are substituted for each other). Once the point is established, a 7 wins for the Don't Pass and the appearance of the point loses for the Don't Pass.

Don't Place: A Place bet against a number, where a 7 wins and the number loses.

Double Odds: A game that offers 2X Odds behind the Pass Line, Don't Pass, Come, and Don't Come.

Double Flips: One die goes to the left or right two times while the other die stays in the original set. This double flip will result in a 7.

Double Pitch: One die spins twice after landing, while staying on axis. On the Hardway set a double pitch automatically ends in a 7.

Down: Bet is taken off the number and is given back to the player. Can be done with all Place bets but not with the contract bets of the Pass Line or Come.

Down Behind: A dealer announces that a Darksider's Don't bet has lost.

Down with Odds: A player's Place number hits and his Come bet goes to the number. This means the Odds are put on the Come and the rest of the Place bet is given back.

Drop Box: Where the player's money is put when he cashes into a game to get his chips.

Easy Way: Numbers not made with doubles. Also known as Soft Way.

Even Money: A bet that is paid off one to one, such as the Pass Line, Come, Don't Pass, and Don't Come. Also known as Flat bet.

Expected Win Rate or Expected Win or Expectation: What the math shows you will either win or lose in the long run based upon how you bet.

Eye in the Sky: Video surveillance area above the casino floor.

Fever: The 5.

Field Bet: Betting on the numbers 2, 3, 4, 9, 10, 11, and 12 at once. If any of these are hit, the bet wins. If the 5, 6, 7, or 8 appears, the bet loses. On layout, the Field is just above the Pass Line.

Fig Vig: Buy bets that collect the commission (also called the "vig" or "vigorish") only on winning bets.

Fire Bet: A bet that the shooter will establish and make each number as his point during his turn with the dice.

Fixed Dice: Dice that are biased either by design or by accident.

Fixing the Dice: Antiquated term for setting the dice.

Flags: Red, white, and blue chips worth $5,000.

Flat Bet: Bet paid off at even money.

Floor Person: Individual who stands behind one or several box persons in a pit and is in charge of making sure everything is run smoothly. Can also be the person who gives out some comps.

Gaff or Gaffed Game: A rigged gaming device, such as dice.

Gambler's Fallacy: The belief that if deviations from expected behaviors are observed in some random process that these deviations are likely to be evened out by opposite deviations in the future.

Garbage Numbers: The numbers 2, 3, 11, and 12.

George: A player who tips. A player who is easy to deal with.

Giving Odds: The same as Laying odds. Taking the long end of a bet.

Gold: Chips usually worth $5,000.

Golden Touch Craps: The premier school for learning dice control.

Grays: Chips usually worth $5,000.

Greens: Chips usually worth $25.

Grind Joint: A low-level casino that shuns high-roller action.

Gripper: A device sold by Golden Touch to help the player create a perfect grip on the dice.

Hardways: A number that comes up in doubles: 1:1, 2:2, 3:3, 4:4, 5:5, and 6:6.

Hardway Set: A set with Hardway box numbers all around it: 2:2, 3:3, 4:4, and 5:5, with the 6-spot and the 1-spot on the axis. These doubles are called Hard numbers.

Hedging Bets: Using one or more bets to offset the impact of one or more other bets.

High-Low: Betting the 12 and the 2 at the same time.

High Roller: Big bettor.

Holding Pattern: During the 5-Count process, after the 4-count if no Box number is rolled, the 5-Count can't be completed yet and is said to be at "4-count and holding."

Hook or Corner: Where the craps table turns. Area of pyramids under the hook is considered the Mixing Bowl, where the dice tend to be randomized even for controlled shooters.

Hop Bet or Hopping Bet: One-roll bet that a certain number will come up, usually in a certain way such as an 8 with 5:3 or a 10 with 8:2.

Horn Bet and Horn High Bet: Multi-number bet in units of $4 that the 2, 3, 11, or 12 will be rolled. $5 variation allows a $2 bet on any of the four numbers. This is called a Horn High bet.

House Edge: The percentage of each bet that the house keeps. House does this by winning more bets than the player or by taxing the players' wins by not paying off at correct odds.

In and In For: How much the player has cashed in for.

In Control of Tip: Player puts down a tip for the dealers and says, "I control it." This means when the bet wins, the dealers can only take down the winning portion, not the original bet.

Independent Trial Game: All the previous decisions at the game have no influence or bearing on what is coming up next.

Inside Numbers: The 5, 6, 8, and 9.

Jimmy "Hicks": The number 6.

Juice: Another term for casino edge. Also a term for high-rolling player who gets what he wants in terms of comps.

Juice Joint: A casino that cheats.

Lay or Lay Bet: To bet against a number at craps and for the 7. Player pays long end of the odds on such bets.

Laying Odds: When the Darkside bet is up on the number, the player may put Odds on the bet. Player puts long end of the Odds since he is betting that the 7 will show. The 7 has an edge against every number and is the favorite to show.

Lightside and Lightsiders: Overwhelming majority of craps players bet with the Pass Line at the game. The Pass Line is a Lightside bet. Lightside players bet with the numbers and against the 7 during the point cycle of the game. Also called Rightside players.

Little Joe or Little Joe from Kokomo: The number 4.

Live One: A player who tips. Also known as a George.

Lock the Chips: Bets or extraneous chips that no one claims are taken by the casino.

Low Roller: Small bettor.

Mantra: Sound that is repeated in one's mind to get a person into an alpha state of consciousness.

Markers: Casino credit. Is essentially a check to the casinos for borrowed money and has a specific time frame in which to be paid back.

Martingale: Betting increasingly more money when you are losing to make up for previous losses. Also known as a Negative Progression. Most players will double their bets after losses, thinking, *I have to win at least one bet*.

Maximum Bets or Table Maximum: The most a player can wager on one bet at a given table.

Midnight: The 12.

Minimum Bets or Table Minimum: The least a player can wager on one bet at a given table.

Mixing Bowl: Where the craps table wall turns in the corners of the table and where the dice tend to be randomized even for controlled shooters.

Monetary Edge: The player's expectation in the game coupled with comps gives the player more money than he loses.

Money Plays: Playing with real money instead of chips.

Monster Roll: A long roll.

Nailing a Player: Catching a player cheating.

Natural: A 7 or 11 on the come-out roll or on the initial placement of a Come bet.

Negative Progressions: Betting increasingly more money when you are losing to make up for previous losses. Also called Martingale.

Nickel: A $5 bet.

Nina Ross and the Bucking Horse: The number 9.

Ninety Days: The number 9.

No Bet: Late bet that is not accepted by the dealers.

No Roll: A roll that does not count.

Odds: The likelihood of something happening against the likelihood of that something not happening. The 7 will come up six times for every three times the 4 will come up. The odds are 6-to-3, or 2-to-1. The Odds bet in craps can be placed on a Pass Line, Don't Pass, Come, and Don't Come bets and are paid off at their true value. For example, a 4 would pay 2-to-1 on the Pass Line and on the Don't Pass it would pay 1-to-2.

Odds Working: On the come-out roll the Odds can work on all Come and Don't Come bets if the player desires.

Off: Odds and Place bets can be turned off, which means the bet is not working and can neither be won nor lost.

Off Axis: Dice fall to the side and do not land on any of the set numbers but on the numbers that can be used with the side pips. In the Hardway set the side pips are the 1-pip and the 6-pip.

On Axis: Dice remain on the pips that are primary. On the Hardway set these would be the 2-pip, 3-pip, 4-pip, and 5-pip.

Opposition Stance: Right-hand shooters standing at stick right; left-handed shooters standing at stick left.

Outside Numbers: The 4, 5, 9, and 10.

Over Seven or Under Seven: The player can bet that the next roll will either go over 7 or under a 7. If a 7 is hit, the bet loses.

Parley: Letting the win and the initial bet ride on the next decision.

Pass and Passers: The shooter is making his Pass Line points. The term for a shooter who makes his Pass Line points.

Passing the Dice: Player prefers not to shoot the dice and passes them to the next player.

Pass Line: Player is betting that the 7 or 11 will win on the come-out roll and that the shooter's point will be made before the 7 is rolled.

Past Posting: Making a bet after the decision has been called. This is the most common form of cheating.

Pay Behind: Dealer call to pay off Don't bets.

PC: Abbreviation for percentage.

Pendulum Swing: Right-handers standing at stick left; left-handers standing at stick right. The swing looks like a pendulum as it takes place.

Phoebe or Little Phoebe: The number 3.

Pig Vig: Buy bets where the commission (vig) must be paid on all wagers, whether they win or lose. House edge is much higher on these than on Fig-Vig Buy bets where commission is only taken out of winning bets.

Pinks: Chips usually worth $2.50.

Pips: White dots or spots on the sides of the dice.

Pit: A group of table games looked over by a Pit Boss.

Pit Boss: The executive in charge of supervising table games in a given Pit.

Pitch Control: The pitch is the possible up-and-down motion of the dice when they are in the air. The more you have such motion the tougher it is to keep the dice under control.

Place Bets or Placing Numbers: Going right up on a number without using the Pass Line or Come; Don't Pass or Don't Come. Casino takes a higher percentage of money from the players for such bets.

Place Odds: Payment of Place bets at "house odds," which means they do not pay off at the true odds of the bet.

Ploppy: Multifaceted term that describes foolish, stupid, idiotic, pathetic dopes, dingbats, and also those who look these parts. Not a compliment. *Ploppy* can be used to describe players, gambling writers, and casino personnel and even people who never go near a casino. It is an all-purpose put-down.

Point: The number the shooter establishes that he must hit before the appearance of the 7 in order for the Pass Line bet to win.

Point Cycle: The part of the craps game where the shooter is looking to make his point on the Pass Line and avoid the 7.

Point Numbers: Also known as Box numbers. The 4, 5, 6, 8, 9, and 10.

Positive Progression: Increasing your bets when you are winning.

Post Holes: The Hard 8.

Power of the Pen: Casino employee who can write comps for the players.

P.O.W.E.R. Plan: How to focus the mind and relax the body in order to get the most out of a physical skill such as dice control. Can be found in the book *Casino Craps: Shoot to Win!*

Press: Increasing one's bet. Usually means doubling it, but the increase can be in any amount.

Pressure: Increasing one's bet.

Primary Hit: Hitting the numbers that your dice are set for. On the Hardway set these would be the hard 4, hard 6, hard 8, and hard 10. On the 3V, these would be 6s and 8s.

Probability: The likelihood that an event or decision will occur.

Progressive Betting: Increasing or decreasing one's bet based on past decisions.

Proposition Bets: High-house-edge bets. Also known as Crazy Crapper bets.

Puck: Black (Off)/white (On) disk that shows whether game is on come-out roll or which Point number has been established by the shooter.

Pumpkins: Orange chips usually worth $1,000.

Puppy Paws: Another name for a hard 10.

Purples: Chips usually worth $500.

Push: A tie.

Put Bets: Placing of a Pass Line or Come Bet with Odds without going through the come-out or initial bet on the come.

Pyramids: Foam-rubber pyramids at the back of the table (also known as the Back Wall) that players' dice should hit with each throw. These are used to help randomize dice throws.

Radical Betting: Using otherwise high-house-edge bets by shooters who have excellent on-axis control of the dice.

Rail: Term in craps for where a player's chips are held during the game.

Railbird: Criminal who steals players' chips from their rails, usually when they are shooting or watching the game and not paying attention to their chips.

Random Rollers: Shooters who have no dice-control skills and shoot the dice with results being determined by randomness. One type of these shooters is called a Chicken Feeder.

Random Rolls: Dice rolls that are determined by randomness and exhibit no control whatsoever.

Rat Hole Chips: Putting chips in your pocket, usually to prevent the casino from knowing how much was won.

Reds: Chips usually worth $5.

RFB: Stands for "Room, Food, and Beverage" and is a term used for high rollers in the casinos. These players get most or all of their expenses comped.

Rhythmic Rollers: Shooters who take care with the dice and with their throw. Early term created by the Captain for dice control, dice influence, and controlled shooting.

Rightside and Right Player: Betting with the point and against the 7 during the point cycle of the game on Pass Line, Come, and Place bets. Also known as Lightside.

Risk Time: The amount of time a player's money is at risk.

RLFB: Stands for "Room, Limited Food [usually non-gourmet], and Beverages." Comp step that is just under RFB.

Same Dice: Many shooters will ask for the same dice when one or both of their dice go off the table. The superstition is that when dice go off the table and the shooter is given new dice, he will seven out.

Save the Odds: When a 7 is rolled on the come-out and the Come bet Odds are not working, these will be returned to the player.

Savvy Players: Smart players who make the best bets at the table in a random game or with novice or intermediate dice controllers.

Secondary Hit: The dice hit a number you are not specifically setting for but that contains one or two of the numbers whose faces are a part of the initial set.

Session: Amount of time a player spends at a table from cashing in to finishing playing.

Seven Out: Call made by the stickman indicating that the Pass Line bet lost and that the dice go to the next shooter. Expression that your roll ended.

Shill: A casino worker who plays games with casino money in order to entice others to play that game.

Single-Point Pop: A die that hits a pyramid directly in its center.

Skinny Dugan: The number 7.

Sleeper: Money left on the table that the player has forgotten about.

Smack!: The sound made when the dice hit the layout flush.

SmartCraps: Software program comprised of three tests to gauge the axis control of a shooter.

Snake Eyes: A 1:1 combination of the dice equaling the number 2.

Soft Way or Soft Bets: Dice combinations not made with doubles.

Split House: Casino where dealers pool their tips.

SRR: Seven-to-Rolls Ratio. A random dice roll averages six 7s for every 36 rolls in the long run. The SRR is therefore 1:6. An SRR above 1:6 or below 1:6 over an extended period of time would probably mean the shooter is influencing the dice.

Stick Left (SL): On the left-hand side of the stickman.

Stick or Stickman: Individual who uses the stick to move the dice to and from the shooter. Individual who calls the numbers when rolled and indicates which Proposition bets have won. Sometimes called Stick Person.

Stick Right (SR): On the right-hand side of the stickman.

Stiff: A player who doesn't tip.

Suits: Those working the pits who wear suits. Generally a negative connotation.

Supersystem: Betting the Do and Don't at the same time. Also called Doey-Don't.

Sweat: Casino personnel who get upset when they lose money or have to deal with savvy players.

Table Dumping: A table losing money.

Tabletop Throw: Shooting the dice from the tabletop before lifting them. Requires more muscle action that a pendulum throw.

Taking Odds: On the Pass or Come putting extra money in play when the number is established. This extra money is called Odds or Free Odds.

Team Play: Groups of players using a combined bankroll to beat the casinos.

Testes Tanking: When a male who is shooting for the first time sevens out quickly.

Texas Sunflowers: The hard 10.

Theoretical Loss: How much a player can expect to lose in the long run betting as he does. This "loss" is the baseline used for comps.

Tip: A gratuity.

Toke: A tip specifically given to a dealer.

Too Tall to Call: A die or both dice land on the chip rail. Also, "In the wood, no good!"

Trend(s): Dice were hitting certain numbers or were missing certain numbers in the recent decisions. In a random game these decisions are meaningless for future decisions.

True Bounce: Bounce that comes from a 45-degree angle on a traditional table.

True Odds: The correct payout based upon the real odds of a bet.

Tub Table: Small, one-dealer craps table that resembles a tub. Players sit to play the game.

Two Ways: Same bet for both the player and the dealer.

Unit or Units: Minimum bet a player makes. If a player's minimum bet is $5, a bet of $10 for him would be a two-unit bet.

Vig: Another name for the casino edge.

Vigorish: Another name for casino edge.

Virgin Principle: The superstition that a woman who has never rolled the dice before will have a good roll.

V Spread: Dice going in opposite directions, causing them to look like a *V* when they have stopped after hitting the back wall. Can be an excellent controlled throw.

Watermelon: Chips worth $25,000.

Whirl or World Bet: A wager that the 2, 3, 7, 11, or 12 will be rolled.

Whites: Chips usually worth $1.

Working Bets: Bets that can be won or lost. Player can have his bets on the various numbers; can work on the come-out roll as can one-roll proposition bets.

Worse Than Random: The mistaken idea that something can be less than random. A dice throw is either random or controlled. There is no such thing as less than random or more than random.

Wrong Side and Wrong Bettor: The Wrong side of a craps game is rooting for the 7 instead of the point during the point cycle of the game. During come-out roll, the Wrong bettor is rooting for the 2 or 3 for a win but does not want a losing 7 or 11 to be rolled. Also called Darkside or Darksider.

Yo: Another term for the 11.

SmartCraps
Training Software
for Dice Controllers

SmartCraps is a fundamentally new way for dice controllers to win at the casino game of craps. With SmartCraps, you will learn:

- How to prove that you are influencing the dice outcomes using our powerful and new ProTest® method or the standard SRR.
- The optimal dice sets and best bets given your unique dice-control skill.
- Your edge over the casino, i.e., how much money you can make playing craps.

Features in SmartCraps:

SmartCraps is crammed with features designed to help dice-control experts maximize their potential wins in the game of craps. Nothing ever developed comes close to the advanced simulators and tools in SmartCraps:

ProTest® Dice-Control Metric: Learn about the ProTest® dice-control test, the most accurate and powerful statistical test for dice control in the game of craps. Instead of needing many thousands of rolls for statistical certainty with tests like the SRR, ProTest® can tell you in a few hundred rolls whether you are in fact influencing the dice.

Dice-Set Optimizer: Use our mathematical calculators to immediately determine the optimal dice set for any craps bets, including Pass and

Don't pass. You'll be amazed to discover what the best dice sets are for you at different points in the game. Prove exactly how much money you can make with your ProTest® dice-control skill!

Professional Craps Simulation: You can model every possible aspect of the game, including rare but important aspects such as Odds, payouts rounding, commission bets (buy bets), multiple shooters, your own betting systems, known and *blind* betting on shooters, Lay bets, random table walkups/shooters, and much more. You can simulate games with SRR shooters, ProTest® dice controllers, or even random shooters.

SRR Support: Run craps simulations with different minimum and/ or maximum SRR values. Find out what edge you have based on your SRR values.

Risk of Ruin (ROR) Calculators and Simulation: Find out how much bankroll you need to survive in any given game with your unique dice-control skill. You can use our ROR simulator to empirically derive your bankroll requirements through multiple simulation sessions. Or you can easily use our ROR calculators that immediately estimate your ROR from well-known mathematical formulas.

Plus Over 100 Pages of Online Help and Documentation: A wealth of detailed help is available at the press of a button in every dialog and at any time. Learn about ProTest®, proof that it works, and even how to take a dice-control test the correct way.

Available for Windows only. **Just $129.95**
www.SmartCraps.com/GTC

Learn the Golden Touch™ from the World's Greatest Dice Controllers

Are you a winner in business—in your chosen job, career, or profession—but a long-term loser at craps? If your answer is yes, it doesn't have to be, because you can learn how to win at craps. Craps *can* be beaten! It isn't easy and not everyone can do it, but then again, not everyone can be successful in business and life. If you are interested in how to win at craps, read on.

There is only one way to beat the game of craps in the long run, and that is through precision dice shooting and perfecting your dice control at the table.

Dice control is a physical skill that can be learned by disciplined players who are willing to practice and perfect the techniques we teach them in our exclusive Golden Touch™ Craps™ dice-control craps seminars. Our teachers are the greatest dice-control specialists in the world, many with books and major publications to their credit, all with years of winning casino experience behind them!

Prominent sports figures, enlightened professionals, and successful businessmen and women take the Golden Touch™ dice-control seminars because you get what you pay for with Golden Touch™:

- Intense one- and two-day craps seminars on the physical elements of controlled shooting: stance and scanning, set, angle, grab, grip, delivery, spin control, and bounce control!
- Hands-on small-group workshops with great coaches who show you how it's done and work side-by-side and step-by-step with you to master the physical elements of dice control.
- Strong tutoring in maintaining mental discipline, focus, centering, and stamina for making your Golden Touch™ last at the craps table no matter what the distractions!
- Betting strategies based on applying sound mathematical principles, rather than superstitions, so that your Golden Touch™ is not tarnished by poor gambling practices!
- How to maintain your edge while random rollers shoot at the table, based on recent breakthrough mathematical research
- How to win the game within the game of casino craps!
- How to assess your edge and optimize your betting strategies to exploit it!

Classes forming now! More info available at www.goldentouchcraps.com
Call us TOLL FREE at 1-866-SET-DICE or 1-800-944-0406

The Golden Touch
Dice-Control DVD

ur brand new two-disc GTC DVD is now ready. ***Golden Touch: Beat Craps by Controlling the Dice*** is a superior, professional product in every way. It is two discs of information, and it is loaded with visuals.

There are **more than 200 controlled throws** shown on the DVD from all angles—front, side, back, tabletop—plus landings, bounces, and back-wall hits. There is also excellent *slow-motion footage* so you can actually see how the dice hit the back wall and land. Some shots go right into the camera from head-on.

Watch four of the best dice controllers in the world and watch them unedited: Frank Scoblete, Dominator, Stickman, and Bill Burton. You will see their shots from every angle from start to finish. You will also be given complete statistics of their throws.

There are no edited shots—you'll see actual practice sessions.

The visuals are remarkable. This two-disc DVD set can be used over and over when you are concerned that your form or throw is somewhat off. The two-disc set costs $299 + $6 for shipping and handling and will be sent priority mail.

Call 1-866-SET-DICE to order by credit card or for more information. Or go to http://www.goldentouchcraps.com/GTCDVD.shtml.